Good Housekeeping's
COOKING WITH SUSAN

By the
Food Editors
of
Good
Housekeeping
Magazine

ILLUSTRATIONS BY
KINUKO CRAFT

PHOTOGRAPHS BY
JAMES VILES AND
WESLEY BALZ

Published by
Consolidated Book Publishers
1727 South Indiana Avenue, Chicago, Illinois 60616

Contents

An Appetizer, 2

Breads, 3
quick breads
yeast breads

Sandwiches, 11

How to pare, cut, cube,
dice, and mince, 14

Salads and Relishes, 16
perky raw relishes

Vegetables, 20

Main Dishes, 21
meat
poultry
fish and shellfish
eggs, cheese, pastas

Cookies, 38

Cakes, 39

Pies, 44

Desserts, 49

Index, 64

An Appetizer

Susan, our perennial teen-age cook, who for more than twenty years has led by the hand, not only teen-agers, but cooks of all ages, starts you off here on a culinary adventure with this easy-to-follow step-by-step recipe for an unusual appetizer.

SHRIMP EGG ROLLS

Shrimp Filling:
1 cup cooked or canned shrimp, chopped
1 cup drained canned bean sprouts, chopped
1 cup finely-chopped celery
½ cup drained canned mushrooms, chopped
1½ teaspoons salt
1 teaspoon monosodium glutamate
½ teaspoon granulated sugar

Egg-Roll Wrappers:
1 cup sifted regular all-purpose flour
1 teaspoon salt
4 eggs, unbeaten
About 2 quarts salad oil

Hot Mustard Sauce:
Cold water
3 tablespoons dry mustard

Make a week ahead, then freezer-wrap and freeze, or day ahead and refrigerate. Or make about 3 hours before serving:

1.   To make Shrimp Filling: Mix together chopped shrimp, bean sprouts, celery, mushrooms, salt, monosodium glutamate, and sugar; refrigerate.

2.   To make batter for Egg-Roll Wrappers: Combine flour, salt, and 3 eggs, beaten. Stir in 1 cup water, a little at a time, until a smooth, thin batter is formed.

3.   To cook Egg-Roll Wrappers: In 7-inch skillet, over medium heat, heat 1 teaspoon salad oil. Pour in 3 tablespoons batter (scant ¼ cup) as in *photo a*. Rotate skillet until batter covers bottom, then cook until surface is set. Do not turn. Carefully slide wrapper onto paper towel as in *photo b*. (If wrapper sticks to pan, roll one edge over and loosen with spatula.)

4.   Wipe any particles from bottom of skillet; repeat step 3 until all of batter is used, cooling each Egg-Roll Wrapper on a piece of paper towel.

5.   To fill egg rolls: Drain Shrimp Filling well. Place 1 heaping tablespoon off-center on one wrapper. Fold two sides over filling; brush exposed surface of wrapper with some of remaining egg, beaten. Starting from filling end, roll up filling in wrapper as in *photo c*. When all egg rolls are filled, refrigerate them, uncovered, 1 hour.

6.   To fry egg rolls: In skillet, heat 1 inch of salad oil to 375°F. on deep-fat-frying thermometer, or until 1-inch square of day-old bread browns in 40 seconds. Fry egg rolls, two at a time, until well-browned on both sides as in *photo d*. Drain on paper towel. (If preferred, refrigerate or freeze after frying, for later use.)

7.   When all egg rolls have been fried, reheat, uncovered, on cookie sheet in 400°F. oven about 10 minutes.

8.   Meanwhile, make Hot Mustard Sauce: Stir enough water into dry mustard to make it the consistency of mayonnaise.

9.   Serve Shrimp Egg Rolls with Hot Mustard Sauce as in *photo e*, before a main dish of frozen or canned chicken chow mein. Complete this Oriental meal with favorite fruit and hot tea. Makes 12 or more egg rolls.

Breads—Quick and Yeast

APRICOT-WALNUT BREAD

½ cup snipped dried apricots
2¼ cups packaged biscuit mix
1 cup uncooked rolled oats
¾ cup granulated sugar
¼ teaspoon salt

1 teaspoon double-acting baking
  powder
1 cup coarsely-broken walnuts
1 egg, well beaten
1¼ cups milk

Make day before:

1. Grease, then flour 9-by-5-by-3-inch loaf pan as in *photo a*.
2. Start heating oven to 350°F.
3. With kitchen scissors, snip apricots onto wax paper as in *photo b*. Measure ½ cup.
4. In large bowl stir biscuit mix with rolled oats, sugar, salt, and baking powder. Stir in apricots and walnuts until well coated as in *photo c*.
5. Into eggs, blend milk with hand beater. Quickly stir into biscuit-mix mixture; with spoon, beat 30 seconds. Turn batter into prepared loaf pan.
6. Bake 1 hour, or until cake tester, inserted in center, comes out clean.
7. Cool in pan 10 minutes; remove to wire rack to cool completely. Let mellow overnight, wrapped in saran or foil. Makes 1 loaf.

Apricot-Walnut Bread

CRISS CROSS CORN BREAD

2 packages corn-muffin mix
1 cup canned salted peanuts
5 frankfurters

Process Cheddar cheese
1 teaspoon whole orégano leaves

About 50 minutes before serving:
1. Assemble all ingredients and utensils as in *photo a.*
2. Start heating oven to 400°F.
3. In large bowl, with rubber spatula, prepare corn-muffin mix, adding milk and eggs as label directs; stir in peanuts. With rubber spatula, spread mixture evenly in greased 13-by-9-by-2-inch ovenglass baking dish.
4. On cutting board, with paring knife, cut frankfurters into diagonal slices, about ½ inch thick, as in *photo b.*
5. Grate cheese onto wax paper as in *photo c;* measure ¼ cup.
6. Over top of corn-muffin mixture, arrange frankfurters, overlapping slices in 5 evenly spaced crosswise rows of 5 slices each, starting at one outer edge almost to center; repeat, starting from opposite side; then, down center, arrange one continuous row of remaining frankfurter slices. Scatter cheese over center row; sprinkle orégano over entire surface.
7. Bake 30 to 35 minutes, or until cake tester, inserted in center, comes out clean.
8. Cool slightly; cut into 10 generous slices. Serve with hot chocolate, topped with whipped cream, as in *photo d.* Top off this snack with a basket of fresh fruits. Makes 10 servings.

BLUEBERRY MUFFINS

1 cup fresh blueberries
Granulated sugar
2 cups sifted regular all-purpose
    flour
3 teaspoons double-acting baking
    powder

1 teaspoon salt
1 egg, unbeaten
1 cup milk
6 tablespoons melted shortening

1. Wash and drain blueberries; pat dry on paper towels. Sweeten to taste with 2 or 3 tablespoons sugar; set aside. (Or use 1 cup frozen blueberries; do not sweeten.)
2. Start heating oven to 425°F.
3. Into bowl sift flour with baking powder, salt, and 2 tablespoons sugar.
4. Beat egg until frothy; add milk and shortening; mix well. Make a small well in center of flour mixture; pour in milk mixture all at once. Stir quickly and lightly—don't beat—*until just mixed, but still lumpy.* Quickly stir in blueberries.
5. Quickly fill 14 greased 2½-inch muffin-pan cups two-thirds full with batter; wipe off any spilled drops. (If batter does not fill all cups, fill empty ones with water to keep grease from burning.) Sprinkle tops of muffins with 4 teaspoons sugar.
6. Bake 25 minutes, or until cake tester, inserted in center of a muffin, comes out clean.
7. Run spatula around each muffin to loosen; lift out into napkin-lined basket and serve piping hot. Makes about 14.
Note: If muffins are done before rest of meal, loosen, then tip in cups; keep warm in pans so they won't steam and soften.

APPLE-CREAM COFFEECAKE

½ cup chopped walnuts
2 teaspoons cinnamon
1½ cups granulated sugar
½ cup butter or margarine
2 eggs, unbeaten
1 teaspoon vanilla extract
2 cups sifted regular
   all-purpose flour

1 teaspoon double-acting
   baking powder
1 teaspoon baking soda
½ teaspoon salt
1 cup commercial sour
   cream
1 medium apple

Early on day:
1. In bowl mix walnuts, cinnamon, and ½ cup sugar.
2. Start heating oven to 375°F.
3. In large bowl, with mixer at high speed, beat butter until creamy; gradually add 1 cup sugar, beating until light and fluffy, and scraping bowl and beaters now and then with rubber spatula. Add eggs, one at a time, then vanilla, beating until blended.
4. Sift flour with baking powder, baking soda, and salt; now, at low speed, beat flour mixture into batter alternately with sour cream. Spread half of batter in well-greased 9-inch tube pan with removable bottom. Top with pared, cored, thinly sliced apple; sprinkle with half of walnut mixture; top with remaining batter, then rest of walnut mixture.
5. Bake 40 minutes, or until cake tester, inserted in center, comes out clean.
6. Remove coffeecake from oven and let stand, in pan, on wire rack 30 minutes. With metal spatula, loosen cake all around side. Then, by top of tube, lift cake, still on base, from pan; let cool on wire rack. Loosen from tube and base, and lift to serving plate. Serve, cut into wedges.

HOT BAKING-POWDER BISCUITS

2 cups sifted regular
   all-purpose flour
3 teaspoons double-acting
   baking powder

1 teaspoon salt
6 to 7 tablespoons
   shortening
⅔ to ¾ cup milk

1. Start heating oven to 450°F.
2. Into bowl, sift flour with baking powder and salt. With pastry blender, or 2 knives, cut in shortening until mixture is like coarse corn meal.
3. Make well in center; pour in ½ cup milk. With fork, mix lightly and quickly. Add enough more milk to form dough that is just moist enough to leave sides of bowl and cling to fork in ball. Turn onto lightly floured surface. Knead gently 6 or 7 times.
4. Lightly roll out dough ½ to ¾ inch thick. With floured 2-inch biscuit cutter, cut out biscuits, using straight, *not twisting*, motion and cutting biscuits close together. With spatula, lift biscuits to ungreased cookie sheet. Place 1 inch apart for crusty biscuits, nearly touching for soft-sided ones. Repeat with trimmings until all dough is used.
5. With pastry brush, brush tops of biscuits with milk, light cream, or melted butter or margarine.
6. Bake 12 to 15 minutes, or until delicate brown. Makes about 19 2-inch biscuits.

Apple-Cream Coffeecake

 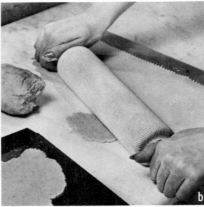 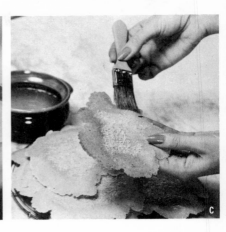

CHEESE CORN CRISPS

1 cup yellow corn meal	3 tablespoons melted
½ cup sifted regular	shortening or salad oil
all-purpose flour	⅓ cup milk
¼ teaspoon baking soda	Shredded Parmesan cheese
½ teaspoon salt	Melted butter or margarine

Make a week or two ahead, or early on day:

1. Start heating oven to 350°F.
2. Sift corn meal with flour, baking soda, and salt. Gradually stir in shortening and milk. On lightly-floured surface, knead the dough, pushing down with heel of hand, turning and repeating 6 to 8 times as in *photo a,* until it just holds together.
3. Break off a nickel-size piece; with stockinet-covered rolling pin, roll into paper-thin, 5-inch round with ragged edges as in *photo b.* Place on ungreased cookie sheet. Repeat until all of dough is used. Sprinkle a little cheese over center of each crisp.
4. Bake 10 to 15 minutes, or until golden.
5. Cool on wire racks; store, covered, in dry place at room temperature.

Just before serving:

Brush each Corn Crisp with some melted butter as in *photo c;* sprinkle with salt. These are delightful with any chicken dish, including curries, chowders, and main-dish salads. Makes 20 to 24.

Before you begin one of Susan's yeast breads, be sure that utensils, work surfaces, and hands are clean. This is a must for good yeast breads. Remember, yeast likes a warm, even temperature. And use only the very best ingredients!

To vary: Omit cheese. Sprinkle celery, poppy, or sesame seeds, or curry or chili powder on crisps after baking and buttering. Or sprinkle with seasoned salt (omitting regular salt).

HOT CROSS BUNS

¾ cup scalded milk	½ teaspoon mace
½ cup shortening	About 3½ to 4 cups sifted
⅓ cup granulated sugar	regular all-purpose flour
1 teaspoon salt	Salad oil
¼ cup warm water	1 egg white, slightly beaten
1 package active dry, or	1 cup confectioners' sugar
cake, yeast	2 tablespoons hot water
1 egg, beaten	½ teaspoon vanilla extract
¾ cup currants	

1. In large bowl combine milk, shortening, granulated sugar, and salt; cool until lukewarm.
2. In small bowl, onto warm water, sprinkle yeast; stir until dissolved. Add to milk mixture with egg, currants, mace, and as much flour as can be stirred into dough—about 3½ cups.
3. Place in greased clean bowl. Brush top with salad oil. Cover with clean towel; let rise in warm place (80°F. to 85°F.) until doubled in bulk—about 2 hours.
4. Turn onto lightly floured surface; knead 1 minute; shape into 18 2-inch balls. In each of 2 greased 8-by-8-by-2-inch pans, arrange 9 balls, about 1 inch apart.
5. With greased kitchen scissors, snip *deep* cross in each bun. Brush with egg white. Cover with towel; let rise in warm place until doubled in bulk.
6. Start heating oven to 425°F.
7. Bake buns 25 minutes, or until done.
8. Cool on wire rack; fill in cross on each bun with combined confectioners' sugar, hot water, and vanilla. Makes 1½ dozen.

To vary: With egg and milk in buns, add 3 tablespoons finely snipped preserved orange or lemon peel and 3 tablespoons citron.

NO-KNEAD RAISIN LOAF

1 cup regular or quick-cooking
  rolled oats
½ cup light molasses
⅓ cup shortening
1 tablespoon salt
2 packages active dry, or cakes,
  yeast

2 eggs, beaten
2 cups seedless raisins
About 5½ cups sifted regular
  all-purpose flour, or 5½ cups
  instant-type flour (do not sift)
¾ cup confectioners' sugar

Early on day:

1. In 3-quart bowl combine 1½ cups boiling water, oats, molasses, shortening, and salt. Let mixture cool until *lukewarm.*
2. Sprinkle yeast onto ½ cup warm water; stir until dissolved.
3. To oat mixture add yeast, eggs, and raisins. With wooden spoon, stir in flour, a cup at a time, until dough is moist and smooth. Cover bowl with wax paper; refrigerate 2 hours.
4. Meanwhile, grease a 3-quart round glass casserole; set aside. When dough has chilled, remove from bowl to floured board. Then, with well-greased hands and without kneading, round and shape loaf; place in greased glass casserole. Let rise, covered, in warm place (80°F. to 85°F.) until doubled (about 1 to 1½ hours), or until a finger, pressed into top as in *photo a,* leaves an indention.
5. Meanwhile, start heating oven to 350°F.
6. Bake loaf 1 hour and 10 minutes, or until cake tester, inserted in center, comes out clean.
7. Let loaf cool on wire rack, in casserole, 10 minutes, then turn out onto wire rack and let cool completely right-side up.
8. Combine confectioners' sugar with 4 teaspoons water. Drizzle icing over top of cooled loaf as in *photo b.* Makes 1 large loaf.

No-Knead Raisin Loaf

WONDERFUL CHEESE BREAD

1½ cups warm water
2 packages active dry, or 1 cake, yeast
2 tablespoons granulated sugar
2¼ teaspoons salt

6¼ to 6½ cups sifted regular all-purpose flour
2 eggs, beaten with fork
2 cups grated process sharp cheese
¼ cup caraway seeds
Melted butter or margarine

Early on day:

1. In large bowl, onto warm water, sprinkle yeast; stir in sugar and salt until dissolved. Add 2 cups flour; beat well with spoon. Add slightly beaten eggs, cheese, and caraway seeds as in *photo a*; beat well. Beat in 4 more cups flour to make a soft dough, using hands if necessary to work it in.

2. Turn dough onto lightly floured surface; cover with inverted bowl; let rest 10 minutes. Now, with heels of hands—not fingers—as in *photo b*, into dough knead enough more of remaining flour, a small amount at a time, to produce a smooth, elastic dough with small blisters under its surface; this takes about 10 minutes.

3. Place dough in large greased bowl, turning it to grease all sides. Cover with clean towel; let rise in warm place (80°F. to 85°F.) until doubled in bulk—about 1½ hours.

4. Now punch down dough by gently pressing fist into center as in *photo c*; let rise again until almost doubled. Punch down; turn out onto light floured surface. Cover with inverted bowl; let rest 10 minutes.

5. With sharp knife, divide dough into four equal parts. With palms of hands, roll each part into a roll 12 inches long. Twist two rolls together like a rope so they are entwined as in *photo d*; seal ends carefully. Lay in greased 9-by-5-by-3-inch loaf pan against one side. Repeat with other two rolls; lay in second greased loaf pan. Cover loaves with

Wonderful Cheese Bread

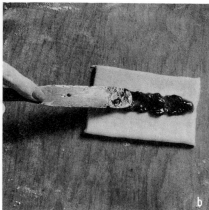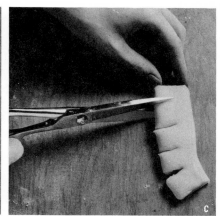

towel; let rise until almost doubled—30 to 45 minutes.
6.   Start heating oven to 350°F.
7.   When loaves have doubled in bulk, brush tops with melted butter as in *photo e, page 8.* Bake 35 minutes, or until done. Loaves should sound hollow when tapped with finger.
8.   Carefully remove loaves from pans; brush tops with more melted butter; cool on side on wire rack, away from draft. Serve, sliced, for dinner, toasted for breakfast, or for sandwiches. Or freezer-wrap in foil; freeze for later use. Makes 2 loaves.

FABULOUS REFRIGERATOR ROLLS

¾ cup milk	*1 egg, unbeaten*
½ cup granulated sugar	*4½ cups sifted regular*
1 teaspoon salt	*all-purpose flour*
½ cup butter or margarine	*Red raspberry or apricot*
¼ cup warm water	*preserves*
1 package active dry, or	*1 egg, beaten*
cake, yeast	

Make dough day before, or early on day:
1.   In small saucepan, scald milk until small bubbles form around edges. Remove from heat; stir in sugar, salt, and butter; cool until lukewarm.
2.   In large bowl, onto warm water, sprinkle yeast; stir until dissolved.
3.   Add lukewarm-milk mixture, unbeaten egg, and one-half of flour to yeast; with mixer at medium speed, beat until smooth. With wooden spoon, beat in remaining flour. Cover bowl tightly with foil; refrigerate at least 2 hours, or up to 3 days.
For Butter Horns:
1.   About 2 hours before serving, cut off amount of dough desired; on floured surface, roll out dough to 10-inch round, ⅛ inch thick. Cut into about 12 wedges.
2.   Spread each wedge lightly with preserves, then roll up as in *photo a.* Place, point side down, on greased cookie sheet.

For Cocks' Combs:
1.   About 2 hours before serving, cut off amount of dough desired; on floured surface, roll out to rectangle ⅛ inch thick.
2.   Cut into rectangles 3 inches by 4 inches. Spread center of each rectangle with preserves as in *photo b.* Fold each in half lengthwise; press edges together. With kitchen scissors, make 4 crosswise cuts in each, halfway across, as in *photo c.*
3.   Place rolls on greased cookie sheet; curve them slightly so cuts fan open. Reroll trimmings and repeat, making more Cocks' Combs.
When rolls are shaped:
1.   Place cookie sheets in warm place (80°F. to 85°F.); let rolls rise until doubled in bulk—about 50 minutes to 1 hour.
2.   Start heating oven to 350°F.
3.   When rolls have doubled, brush tops with beaten egg.
4.   Bake 15 minutes, or until golden.
5.   Remove from pans; serve hot for brunch or as an afternoon snack. Makes about 2 dozen.

LEMON BUBBLE LOAF
(Pictured on page 10)

1 cup granulated sugar	*3 packages active dry, or*
¼ teaspoon mace	*cakes, yeast*
Grated peel of 2 lemons	*2 eggs, well beaten*
1 cup milk	*5¾ to 6¼ cups sifted*
1 teaspoon salt	*regular all-purpose flour*
¼ cup butter or margarine	*2 tablespoons melted butter*
½ cup warm water	*or margarine*

Early on day:
1.   In small bowl combine ½ cup sugar, mace, and lemon peel; set aside.
2.   In small saucepan, scald milk until tiny bubbles appear around edges. Stir in ½ cup sugar, salt, and ¼ cup butter; cool until lukewarm.

3. In very large bowl, onto warm water, sprinkle yeast; stir until dissolved. Stir in milk mixture, eggs, and 3 cups flour, beating all until smooth.

4. Into mixture, stir 2½ cups more flour, or enough to make a soft dough that just cleans sides of bowl. Sprinkle flat surface with half of remaining flour; turn dough onto it, then knead as in *photo b, page 8,* until dough is smooth and elastic, with small blisters under its surface.

5. Place dough in large greased bowl, turning to grease on all sides. Cover with clean towel; let rise in warm place (80°F. to 85°F.) until doubled in bulk—about 45 minutes.

6. Into center of dough, poke 2 fingers about 1-inch deep as in *photo a.* If they leave an indentation, punch down dough as in *photo c, page 8.* Now turn dough onto floured surface; cover with inverted bowl and let rest 10 minutes.

7. Cut dough in half; cut each half into 16 equal pieces. Shape each piece into a ball, tucking any ends under as in *photo b.* Place 16 balls in a layer in greased 15½-by-4½-by-4½-inch angel-loaf pan as in *photo c.* Brush with half of melted butter; sprinkle with half of lemon-mace mixture. Repeat with remaining dough.

8. Cover loaf with towel; let rise in warm place until doubled in bulk —about 45 minutes.

9. Start heating oven to 350°F.

10. Bake loaf 35 minutes, or until done. It should sound hollow when tapped with finger.

11. Cool in pan 5 minutes; turn out on wire rack to cool completely. Makes 1 large loaf.

Lemon Bubble Lo

Sandwiches— hot and cold

BARBECUED-BEEF BUNS

¼ cup vinegar	½ cup butter or margarine
1½ cups water	1 cup catchup or chili sauce
¼ cup granulated sugar	3 tablespoons Worcester-
4 teaspoons prepared	shire
mustard	4 cups 2-inch strips cooked
¼ teaspoon pepper	beef (leftover pot roast)
¼ teaspoon cayenne pepper	Celery, sliced on an angle
1 tablespoon salt	Pitted ripe olives
2 thick lemon slices	About 20 hamburger buns,
2 medium onions, sliced	split and toasted

Early on day:
In Dutch oven combine vinegar, water, sugar, mustard, peppers, salt, lemon slices, onion slices, and butter; simmer, uncovered, 20 minutes. Add catchup, Worcestershire, and pot-roast strips; refrigerate.
About 45 minutes before serving:
1. Let beef mixture simmer slowly until heated. Then, for a bright touch, sprinkle top with celery and ripe olives.
2. Let guests spoon this savory barbecued-beef mixture between split, toasted buns (buttered, if desired). Makes 8 hearty servings.

HAMBURGER STROGANOFF BUNS

¼ cup butter or margarine	1 pound fresh mushrooms,
½ cup minced onion	sliced
1 pound chuck, ground	1 10½-ounce can
1 clove garlic, minced	condensed cream-of-
2 tablespoons regular	chicken soup, undiluted
all-purpose flour	6 hard rectangular bakers'
2 teaspoons salt	or baked brown 'n' serve
¼ teaspoon monosodium	club rolls
glutamate	1 cup commercial sour
¼ teaspoon pepper	cream
¼ teaspoon paprika	Snipped parsley, chives, or
	fresh dill

1. In hot butter in skillet, sauté onions until golden. Stir in chuck, garlic, flour, salt, monosodium glutamate, pepper, paprika, and mushrooms; sauté 5 minutes. Add soup; simmer, uncovered, 10 minutes.
2. Meanwhile, cut thin slice from top of each roll; hollow out rolls.

3. Stir sour cream into meat mixture. (Do not allow to boil.) Fill rolls with this Stroganoff; sprinkle with parsley, chives, or dill. Serve rolls with spiced peaches. Makes 6 servings.

WAFFLE DEVILS

8 bread slices	1 3-ounce package cream
1 2¼-ounce can deviled	cheese
ham	Melted butter or margarine

1. Preheat waffle iron as manufacturer directs. Spread half of bread slices with deviled ham; spread other half with cream cheese. Put together sandwich-fashion, then brush both sides with melted butter.
2. Toast in waffle iron until golden brown. Makes 4 servings.

PARTY SANDWICH LOAF

Fillings, page 12	⅓ to ½ cup light cream
½ 5-ounce jar sharp-cheese	1 day-old loaf unsliced
spread	white bread
2 tablespoons hot water	6 thin tomato slices
3 3-ounce packages soft	Radish slices
cream cheese	Snipped parsley
¼ pound Danish blue	
cheese	

Night before, if convenient:
Prepare any 3 of the fillings as directed; *refrigerate at once.*
Early on day:
1. Blend sharp-cheese spread with hot water. Blend cream cheese and blue cheese with enough cream to spread easily.
2. With sharp knife, trim all crusts from bread. Lay loaf on side and slice lengthwise into 5 even slices, about ½-inch thick. (Use a ruler as a guide to keep slices straight.)
3. Spread bottom bread slice with sharp-cheese spread. Spread second bread slice with half of Chicken Salad (or fish or shellfish salad) filling; top with tomato slices, trimming them with sharp knife so they cover filling evenly; top with rest of Chicken Salad. Place on cheese-spread slice.
4. Spread third bread slice with Egg Salad filling; place on Chicken Salad layer. Avoid pressing layers together too firmly, lest fillings ooze.
5. Spread fourth bread slice with Ham Salad filling; place on Egg Salad layer. Top loaf with last bread slice, with rounded side up; gently shape loaf with hands so all sides are even. Remove any oozing bits.
6. With spatula, frost top and sides with cream cheese-blue cheese spread. Refrigerate several hours, or until easy to cut.
7. To serve, top loaf with sliced radishes; sprinkle

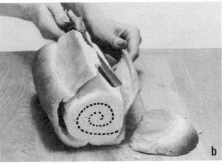

with parsley. With sharp knife, cut into 10 1-inch slices. Cake server makes serving easy. Makes 10 servings.

Fillings (*choose any three*):

HAM SALAD: Mix ½ cup ground cooked or canned ham, or chopped canned ham or luncheon meat with 2 tablespoons minced green pepper, 1 teaspoon prepared mustard, 2 tablespoons mayonnaise, and 1 tablespoon minced onion. Refrigerate.

CHICKEN SALAD: Mix ½ cup ground or finely chopped cooked or canned boned chicken or turkey with ¼ cup minced celery, 2 tablespoons pickle relish, ½ teaspoon salt, dash pepper, and 2 tablespoons mayonnaise. Add a pinch of curry powder, if desired. Refrigerate.

TUNA, SALMON, OR CRAB SALAD: Substitute flaked fresh or canned fish or shellfish for chicken or turkey in Chicken Salad, above. Refrigerate.

EGG SALAD: Mix 2 finely chopped hard-cooked eggs with 2 tablespoons minced ripe olives, ½ teaspoon salt, dash pepper, ½ to ¾ teaspoon prepared mustard, and 2 tablespoons mayonnaise. Refrigerate. *Note:* Canned deviled ham may be substituted for Ham Salad, above.

PINWHEEL SANDWICH LOAF

1 pound frankfurters
1 cup canned pork and beans
½ cup catchup
¼ cup pickle relish

1 loaf unsliced bakery bread
Butter or margarine, softened
Parsley
Bottled barbecue sauce

Early on day:

1. Simmer franks in water 5 minutes; set one aside. With French knife, slice rest, then chop as in *photo a*. Mix chopped franks with beans, catchup, and relish.
2. With long, narrow bread knife, cut crusts from bread as in *photo b*, then trim edges to make loaf cylindrical. Cut loaf pinwheel-style, starting from outside, and, with knife parallel to length of loaf, carefully cut around to center as dotted lines in *photo b* indicate.
3. Gently unroll loaf and spread with butter; top with frank mixture. Reroll loaf as in *photo c*; wrap in wax paper and refrigerate.

Pinwheel Sandwich Loaf

Hot Corned-Beef Barbecues

About 20 minutes before serving:
1. Start heating oven to 400°F.
2. Melt 2 tablespoons butter. Place roll on cookie sheet; brush with melted butter. Bake 10 minutes.
3. Transfer sandwich loaf to platter; garnish with reserved frankfurter, sliced diagonally, and parsley. Cut into 1-inch slices. Serve with barbecue sauce. Makes 7 to 9 servings.

HOT CORNED-BEEF BARBECUES

1 teaspoon chili powder	¾ cup catchup
2 tablespoons cider vinegar	¾ cup water
2 tablespoons Worcestershire	2 12-ounce cans corned beef
⅛ to ¼ teaspoon cayenne pepper	8 hamburger buns, split
	8 whole sweet pickles

About 30 minutes before serving:
1. Over wax paper, accurately measure chili powder as in *photo a*. Place in skillet with vinegar and Worcestershire; add cayenne pepper to taste.
2. Using ½- and ¼-cups of measuring set, measure catchup as in *photo b*. Stir into seasonings in skillet. Now, with liquid measuring cup at eye level, measure water. Stir into catchup mixture.
3. Stir in corned beef, breaking it up with a wooden spoon as in *photo c*. Cook, uncovered, over medium heat, stirring occasionally, about 20 minutes, or until most of liquid has evaporated and corned-beef mixture is thick.
4. Meanwhile, preheat broiler 10 minutes, or as manufacturer directs. Place hamburger buns, split side up, on cookie sheet; broil, 4 inches from heat, about 2 minutes, or until lightly toasted.
5. Spoon corned-beef mixture onto bottom half of toasted buns; put on tops. Garnish each with a sweet pickle on a wooden pick as pictured. Serve with large glasses of cold milk. Makes 8 servings.

Top row: To pare vegetables—rinse; with vegetable parer remove thin layer of skin. Remove any blemishes. To seed green pepper—cut around center stem; lift out. Rinse inside. To peel onion — slit skin from stem to root end; slip off one or two layers of skin. To make carrot sticks—cut pared carrot in half crosswise; cut each half into lengthwise slices. Stack every two slices; cut series of lengthwise sticks. To cut "Chinese style"—rinse vegetables; scrub with brush if sandy. Cut, on diagonal, into thin slices. *Second row*: To cube, dice, mince, or cut into strips — green pepper shown is cubed (about ½ inch), diced (about ¼ inch), and minced (about ⅛ inch). Strips can be any size. To cube sweet potatoes—rinse, pare

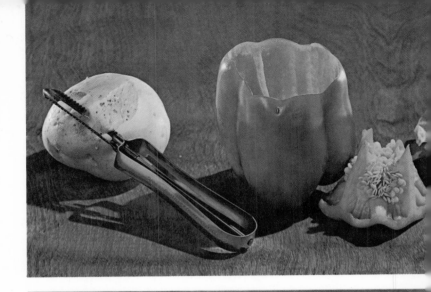

How to pare, cut, cube, dice, and mince

thinly. With knife, cut into slices; stack two slices; cut through them as pictured. To dice zucchini — scrub, do not pare. With paring knife, cut into lengthwise slices. Make lengthwise slits almost to end of each slice; cut across slits. *Bottom row*: To chop or mince with French knife —with 2 or 3 fingers press down on back of blade, near point. With handle in other hand, cut up and down, in rocking motion, pivoting knife. To mince an onion—peel, then make a series of cuts lengthwise and crosswise, some distance down into onion Cut down through, as pictured, into tiny squares. To shred beets—wash; cut a thin slice from both ends, then pare with vegetable parer. Rub beet across grater of desired coarseness, grating onto board or wax paper. To snip parsley—rinse in cold water, shake dry. Place in measuring cup; snip with kitchen scissors to desired degree of fineness.

Salads and Relishes

COLESLAW

4 cups finely shredded green or Chinese cabbage	1/3 cup slivered green pepper or raw green beans
1 tablespoon minced onion	1/3 cup grated carrot
1/3 cup diced celery	1/4 cup sliced radishes
	Coleslaw Dressing, below

Gently toss vegetables together, then toss with Coleslaw Dressing. Refrigerate until ready to serve. Makes 4 servings.

To vary: Substitute 1/2 cup diced tomatoes for carrot and radishes.

COLESLAW DRESSING: Blend 1/2 cup mayonnaise or cooked salad dressing with 3/4 teaspoon salt, dash pepper, dash paprika, 1/2 teaspoon granulated sugar, 1 tablespoon vinegar or lemon juice, and 1 tablespoon milk. Refrigerate. Makes 1/2 cup.

OLIVE COLESLAW

4 cups finely shredded green or Chinese cabbage	1/2 cup sliced stuffed olives
	1 tablespoon minced onion
3/4 teaspoon celery seeds	Coleslaw Dressing, above

Toss cabbage with celery seeds, olives, and onion. Toss with dressing. (You may add 5 coarsely grated frankfurters, if desired.) Refrigerate. Makes 4 servings.

WALDORF COLESLAW

4 cups shredded green or Chinese cabbage	1/2 cup light or dark raisins or grapes, or diced oranges, pineapple, or peaches
1/4 cup broken nut meats	
1/2 cup diced unpared apple	
	Coleslaw Dressing, above

Toss cabbage with nuts and fruits. Then toss with Coleslaw Dressing. Refrigerate. Makes 4 servings.

CALICO COLESLAW

5 cups shredded green cabbage	1/2 teaspoon dry mustard
1/4 cup minced green pepper	1/2 teaspoon grated onion
1/4 cup shredded carrot	2 tablespoons granulated sugar
1 teaspoon salt	
1/4 teaspoon pepper	2 tablespoons salad oil
	1/3 cup vinegar

Place cabbage, green pepper, and carrot in bowl. Combine salt, pepper, mustard, onion, sugar, salad oil, and vinegar. Pour over cabbage; toss until well mixed. Refrigerate. Makes 4 servings.

CHOPPED COLESLAW

3 cups chopped green cabbage	2 tablespoons granulated sugar
1/4 cup chopped green pepper	1 tablespoon chopped pimento
1 teaspoon salt	1 teaspoon grated onion
1/4 teaspoon pepper	3 tablespoons salad oil
1/2 teaspoon dry mustard	1/3 cup vinegar
1 teaspoon celery salt	Sliced olives or tomatoes

Toss cabbage with green pepper, salt, pepper, mustard, celery salt, sugar, pimento, onion, salad oil, and vinegar. Garnish with sliced olives or tomatoes. Refrigerate. Makes 4 servings.

CRACKER CRISP SALAD

About 1 quart crisp salad greens (iceberg, Bibb, or Boston lettuce, romaine, escarole, endive, etc.)	1 tablespoon wine vinegar
	1/4 teaspoon Worcestershire
	1 1-pound can salmon; or 1 6½- or 7-ounce can tuna, drained; or 1 can boned chicken (1 cup)
2 to 4 tomatoes, peeled	
1 clove garlic	6 to 8 radishes, sliced
3/4 teaspoon salt	1 cup packaged small cheese crackers
1/2 cup mayonnaise or cooked salad dressing	

Just before serving:

1. Tear salad greens into bite-size pieces right in salad bowl. Slice tomatoes vertically, with stem ends down. (This way they lose less juice, salad doesn't get watery.) Cut half of tomato slices into chunks; add chunks to greens.
2. With fork, mash garlic with salt until garlic disintegrates. Combine with mayonnaise, vinegar, and Worcestershire; set aside.
3. Break salmon into large chunks over greens; scatter on radish slices and cheese crackers. Pour on dressing; toss to coat well. Garnish with tomato slices. Makes 4 generous servings.

OLD-FASHIONED LETTUCE BOWL

2 medium heads Boston lettuce	1 teaspoon granulated sugar
	1/4 teaspoon salt
1/2 cup light cream	3 or 4 scallions
1/4 cup vinegar	

1. Wash, then refrigerate heads of lettuce, as soon as they come from grocer's.
2. Make dressing right in measuring cup: To cream in cup, add vinegar, sugar, and salt; stir until blended. Refrigerate.

3. At mealtime, with kitchen scissors, snip lettuce into bite-size pieces right in salad bowl. Snip scallions over lettuce. Refrigerate until needed.

Just before serving:
Toss salad with dressing to coat well. Makes 4 servings.

MELON BOAT SALAD

½ cup cottage cheese
2 tablespoons crumbled
   Danish blue cheese, or
   ½ 3-ounce package
   cream cheese
1 large cantaloupe,
   honeydew, or Spanish
   melon

1 pint strawberries
2 oranges
2 bananas
¼ cup chopped walnuts
Bottled French dressing
   (optional)

About 1 hour and 30 minutes before serving:

1. In small bowl mix cottage cheese with blue cheese; refrigerate.
2. Quarter melon; remove seeds. Press cup side of melon-baller into melon, twist, and scoop out melon ball as in *photo a*. Place in bowl. Repeat until as much melon as possible has been made into balls. Then, with spoon, scrape out excess melon (use as nibbler); refrigerate melon balls and shells.
3. Rinse strawberries; hull and halve all but 4; refrigerate.
4. With sharp knife, section oranges: Pare skin, like an apple, cutting deep enough to remove white membrane. Now, go over oranges again, removing any bits of white membrane. Cut alongside each dividing membrane from outside to core. Remove sections as in *photo b*. Place in bowl. When all have been removed, squeeze juice from membranes into same bowl.
5. Peel bananas; score lengthwise with 4-tined fork as in *photo c*. Slice on diagonal; mix with orange sections and juice in bowl—the acid of juice helps to prevent discoloration.
6. Place melon shells on salad plates; arrange melon balls, strawberry halves, orange sections, and banana slices in each.
7. Form cheese mixture into 4 balls; roll in chopped walnuts. Place one on each salad. Garnish each with a whole strawberry. Refrigerate until serving time.
8. Serve as luncheon main dish with hot rolls. Pass bottled dressing. Makes 4 servings.

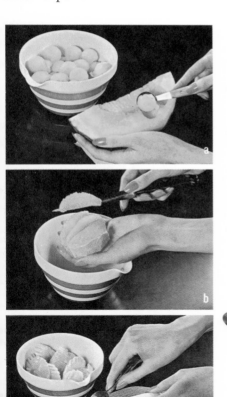

Melon Boat Salad

Radish Roses

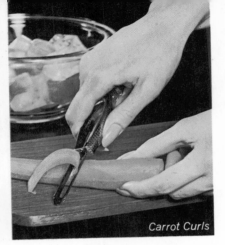

Carrot Curls

Celery Fans

Fluted Cucumber Slices

Relish Tray

Radish Roses: From each radish cut all but one small leaf. From root end, cut two narrow wedges, one crossing the other. Next, make two cuts, one behind the other as pictured, repeating these 3 times around radish. Place finished radish rose in ice water until petals open as shown.

Carrot Curls: Pare large, crisp carrots. Then, holding each as pictured, use vegetable parer to shave off lengthwise strips. Roll each strip around finger. Place in bowl of ice cubes until ready to serve.

Perky Raw Relishes

Celery Fans: Cut celery stalks into 3-inch lengths. Make several parallel slits in each end almost to center as pictured. Or make all slits in same end almost to opposite end. Place celery in a bowl of ice water until slits fan out.

Fluted Cucumber Slices: Score an unpared cucumber by running a sharp-tined fork down length of cucumber from one end to other. Make thin crosswise slices as pictured and refrigerate until needed.

Radish Fans: Cut each radish into thin slices almost through to other side. Place in bowl of ice water until they fan out.

Olive Sticks: Stuff pitted ripe and green olives with thin sticks of carrot and celery; place in refrigerator until ready to serve.

Relish Tray: Arrange all crisp relishes on serving platter as pictured; serve with meat course; no separate salad or salad course is necessary. Serve a tiny pitcher of Italian or other favorite salad dressing for those who like to dunk the relishes.

DEVILED EGGS

6 eggs
¼ cup mayonnaise
1 teaspoon dry mustard
¼ teaspoon salt

Pinch pepper
Several dashes Tabasco
Fresh dill sprigs or radish slices
   (optional)

Several hours ahead:

1.   Hard-cook eggs: Set unshelled eggs out about 1 hour to come to room temperature. Place eggs in saucepan; add enough cold water to cover tops by at least 1 inch. Cover saucepan and bring water rapidly to full boil. Immediately remove pan from heat as in *photo a,* or turn heat to very low to prevent further boiling, which might cause yolks to toughen. Let eggs stand in water, covered, 15 minutes.

2.   Cool eggs promptly and thoroughly in cold water to make shells easier to remove and to prevent dark surfaces on yolks. Remove shells by tapping entire surface of each egg until crackled; roll between hands to loosen shell, then peel, starting at large end. Dipping egg into bowl of cold water helps to ease off shell.

3.   Cut shelled eggs into halves lengthwise as in *photo b.* Or, if stand-up deviled eggs are desired, cut off broad end through yolk, also cut a thin slice from tip end, so egg will stand erect as in *photo c.* Carefully remove yolks to small bowl; set whites aside.

4.   Mash yolks with fork until very fine and crumbly; then blend in mayonnaise, mustard, salt, pepper, and Tabasco. Generously fill hollows in whites with yolk mixture, slightly rounding each. If desired, garnish eggs with fresh dill or radish slices as pictured, or with pimento strips, ripe olives, green olives, parsley sprigs, or paprika sprinkles. Refrigerate until serving time.

5.   Serve deviled eggs as a salad on salad greens, as a garnish for a main-dish chicken, fish, or vegetable salad, or on a cold-meat platter. Makes 12 deviled-egg halves or 6 stand-up eggs.

WARM DEVILED EGGS: About 25 minutes before serving, start heating oven to 250°F. Place deviled eggs, without garnishes, in a shallow baking dish; cover tightly with foil. Heat 15 minutes. Then garnish as desired and serve as party nibblers. If serving at a buffet, keep eggs warm in chafing dish or on an electric hot tray.

DOUBLE-DEVILED EGGS: For a picnic, double recipe; fill lengthwise halves generously. Put halves back together, sandwich-fashion, and wrap individually in saran as in *photo d.* Arrange eggs in egg carton for easy packing in picnic basket. Makes 12 double-deviled eggs.

SKILLET POTATO SALAD

2 pounds potatoes (6)
6 bacon slices
¼ cup bacon fat
1½ tablespoons regular
   all-purpose flour
1 cup water
⅓ cup vinegar
1¾ teaspoons salt
⅛ teaspoon pepper

1 tablespoon granulated sugar
1 teaspoon prepared mustard
2 celery stalks, sliced
1 small head romaine
1 cucumber, thinly sliced, or 2 cups
   cooked green beans or peas
2 small onions, sliced
6 radishes, sliced

1.   Boil unpared potatoes until *just* tender.

2.   Meanwhile, in cold 10-inch skillet, over low heat, fry bacon until crisp, pouring fat into measuring cup as bacon cooks. Remove skillet

from heat; drain bacon on paper towels; then crumble slices.

3. Return ¼ cup bacon fat to skillet; stir in flour, then water, until smooth; add vinegar, salt, pepper, sugar, and mustard. Cook over low heat, stirring, until thickened; remove from heat.

4. When potatoes are *just* tender, drain; peel, then slice. Put skillet back over low heat; add layer of potato slices, then layer each of celery, romaine, in bite-size pieces, cucumber, and onions, repeating until all are used. Toss gently. Top with radishes and bacon bits. Nice with cold sliced meats and rye bread. Makes 6 servings.

SKILLET LUNCHEON SALAD: Brown 6 frankfurters, sliced diagonally, in bacon fat before stirring in flour, water, etc., in step 3.

PICCALILLI

8 quarts green tomatoes	½ cup salt
12 sweet red peppers	1 cup mustard seeds
12 green peppers	3 tablespoons celery seeds
1 quart small onions	1 tablespoon cinnamon
3 quarts cider vinegar	1 tablespoon allspice
7 cups granulated sugar	

1. Place 12 pint preserve jars on wire rack in deep kettle with cold water to cover their tops by at least 1 inch. Cover; boil jars 20 minutes, caps 5 minutes. Keep in boiling water until ready to be filled.

2. Wash tomatoes; cut out stem ends; quarter lengthwise. Wash and seed peppers; halve, then quarter lengthwise. Peel and quarter onions.

3. Put all vegetables through grinder, using medium-fine blade. Pour vegetables into colander; drain off liquid and discard it.

4. Turn vegetables into large kettle; add 2 quarts vinegar; boil, uncovered, 30 minutes, stirring often. Again drain vegetables, discarding liquid.

5. Into vegetables, stir 1 quart vinegar, sugar, and remaining ingredients. Simmer, uncovered, 3 minutes.

6. Pack at once into sterilized jars to within 1 inch of top. Pour ½-inch layer of hot new paraffin into each. Seal at once as manufacturer directs; cool. Makes about 12 pints.

In home canning, the sterilizing of jars and lids is most important, to prevent dangerous bacteria from forming. So follow the instructions carefully. Many jar manufacturers will supply detailed home-canning information upon request.

Vegetables

BUTTERED CARROT STICKS

1 pound carrots	Dash pepper
Salt	Snipped parsley
Butter or margarine	

1. Scrub carrots. Scrape or pare with vegetable parer; cut into thin sticks.

2. Bring 1 inch water to boil in saucepan. Add ½ teaspoon salt for each cup water; add carrots.

3. Cover pan; bring water back to boil over high heat; reduce heat just enough to keep water boiling. Cook carrots 10 to 14 minutes, or until done as you like them. (Use shorter time for tender-crisp carrots, longer time for well-done carrots.)

4. Spoon carrots into heated serving dish; keep warm. Boil carrot liquid down to 1 or 2 tablespoons; add butter; season with salt and pepper. Add snipped parsley; pour over carrots. Serve immediately. Makes 4 servings.

To vary: Cook 1 cup thinly sliced onions, ½ cup snipped scallions, or diced celery with carrots.

FESTIVE CORN SAUTÉ

8 ears fresh corn*	¼ teaspoon monosodium
¼ cup butter or margarine	glutamate
1 cup thin onion rings	¼ teaspoon dried orégano
½ cup green pepper strips	½ cup light cream
1½ teaspoons salt	2 medium tomatoes, sliced, then halved

1. Select the freshest, tenderest corn possible. Husk and clean it, removing silk carefully. With very sharp knife, on cutting board, cut corn from cob: Starting at top of each ear and cutting toward bottom, slice off kernels, being careful not to cut too close to cob, and cutting enough to measure 4 cups.

2. Melt butter in heavy 10-inch skillet (or chafing dish or electric skillet), over medium heat. Add corn, onion rings, green pepper strips, salt, monosodium glutamate, and orégano. Cook mixture, covered, 6 or 7 minutes, or until corn is just tender. During cooking, shake skillet gently, or remove cover once or twice and stir mixture with wooden spoon.

3. Add cream and tomatoes. Simmer, uncovered, 1 or 2 minutes, or until tomatoes are hot but still firm. Makes 4 to 6 servings.

*If using 2 10-ounce packages frozen whole-kernel corn, broken up, or 2 12-ounce cans corn, drained, start with step 2.

To vary: Add ½ cup sliced stuffed olives, omitting green peppers, tomatoes, and 1 teaspoon salt.

SUSAN'S HASHED BROWNS

4 peeled, chilled, cooked
   medium potatoes
1 tablespoon grated onion
1 teaspoon salt
Dash pepper

3 tablespoons butter or
   margarine
3 tablespoons bacon fat
   or shortening

1. Using medium grater, grate potatoes onto wax paper to measure 4 cups. With same grater, grate onion, then toss with potatoes, salt, and pepper.
2. In 10-inch skillet, over medium-high heat, heat butter with bacon fat. Add potatoes, pressing down well with turner and shaping into circle, leaving ½-inch trough of fat around edge.
3. Sauté about 20 minutes, or until brown and crisp on underside. (After 12 to 15 minutes, lift edge to test brownness.)
4. When potatoes are golden on bottom, hold skillet with one hand; with turner, cut through them from far edge to center. Then, with pancake turner, carefully fold these 2 cut quarters, in turn, toward you, onto uncut half.
5. Carefully run turner under potatoes, so they'll slide out of skillet easily. Then, using turner and holding skillet firmly in one hand, turn potatoes onto platter, with uncut side on top. Makes 4 servings.

SCALLOPED POTATOES

2 tablespoons snipped
   parsley
1½ cups thinly sliced onions
4½ cups thinly sliced,
   pared white potatoes
3 teaspoons salt

3 tablespoons butter or
   margarine
7 teaspoons regular
   all-purpose flour
⅛ teaspoon pepper
⅛ teaspoon paprika
1¾ cups milk

1. Start heating oven to 400°F.
2. In saucepan, bring 1 inch water to boil, covered. Prepare parsley, onions, and potatoes.
3. To boiling water, add onions, potatoes, and 2 teaspoons salt; boil, covered, 5 minutes. Drain.
4. Meanwhile, in double boiler or skillet, over very low heat, melt butter. Stir in flour, 1 teaspoon salt, pepper, paprika, then milk. Cook, stirring constantly, until smooth and thickened.
5. In greased 1½-quart casserole, arrange one third of potatoes and onions; sprinkle with half of parsley; pour on one third of sauce. Repeat with another third of potatoes and onions, rest of parsley, half of remaining sauce. Add rest of potatoes, onions, and sauce.
8. Bake, uncovered, 35 minutes, or until tender and brown. Makes 4 or 5 servings.

Main Dishes

When the dish is prepared to perfection, every family meal becomes a sumptuous banquet. Even gourmet and foreign dishes are not so difficult if you carefully follow Susan's step-by-step directions. Here she gives you a variety of meat, poultry, fish, shellfish, egg, cheese, and pasta dishes, any one of which could be company fare. Remember that seasoning (such as salt, pepper, seasoned salt, etc.) may be adjusted to taste.

BROWN BEEF STEW

⅓ cup regular all-purpose
   flour
¼ teaspoon pepper
½ teaspoon celery salt
2 pounds boned chuck, cut
   into 2-inch pieces
¼ cup fat or salad oil
¼ cup minced onion
1 clove garlic, minced
3 cups hot water
3 beef-bouillon cubes

½ teaspoon salt
½ teaspoon Worcestershire
16 small white onions
8 pared small carrots,
   halved crosswise
1 pound fresh mushrooms,
   thickly sliced
1 8-ounce package medium
   noodles
Snipped parsley

Make stew day before:
1. In bowl combine flour, pepper and celery salt. Drop in meat, a few pieces at a time; toss until well coated. Reserve leftover flour.
2. In hot fat, in Dutch oven or deep kettle, slowly brown floured meat, a few pieces at a time, on all sides —15 to 20 minutes. Remove pieces as they brown.
3. To fat in Dutch oven, add minced onion and garlic; sauté until just tender. Stir in reserved flour until blended. Slowly stir in water, bouillon cubes, salt, and Worcestershire. Add meat. Simmer, covered, over low heat, about 2 hours, or until meat is fork-tender.
4. Add whole onions and carrots; simmer, covered, about 20 minutes. Add mushrooms; simmer, covered, about 10 minutes, or until vegetables are tender. Cool; refrigerate.
About 30 minutes before serving:
1. Cook noodles as label directs; put stew on to heat.
2. On large platter arrange noodles; spoon on stew, then sprinkle with parsley. Makes 6 servings.

MEXICALI MEAT PIE

2 pounds beef round, ground
½ pound smoked ham, ground
¼ pound calf liver, ground
1 teaspoon salt
⅛ teaspoon pepper
1 cup fresh white-bread crumbs
1 tablespoon minced green pepper
2 tablespoons snipped parsley

2 eggs, beaten
⅓ cup catchup
2 tablespoons Worcestershire
Few drops Tabasco
2 tablespoons prepared mustard
¼ cup melted butter or margarine
2 12-ounce cans Mexican-style
  whole-kernel corn

Several hours before serving:
1.   In large bowl combine beef, ham, liver, salt, pepper, crumbs, green pepper, parsley, eggs, catchup, Worcestershire, and Tabasco. With large, 2-tined fork, mix these ingredients together.
2.   Use this meat mixture to line a 10-inch pie plate, making sides 2 inches thick and even. With thumb and forefinger, form rope edge around top, making 16 "ropes" in all as in *photo a*. Refrigerate 1 hour or longer.

About 1 hour before serving:
1.   Start heating oven to 350°F.
2.   Bake pie 30 minutes; drain off liquid. Bake 15 minutes longer; drain again.
3.   Meanwhile, blend mustard with butter. Heat corn, then heap in center of baked pie as in *photo b*. Serve pie in wedges; pass mustard butter. Makes 6 to 8 servings.

Mexicali Meat Pie

MEAT-BALL PIZZAS

1 package active dry, or
   cake, yeast
5 cups sifted regular
   all-purpose flour
1 teaspoon salt
⅓ cup olive oil
½ pound chuck, ground,
   in marble-size balls
2 tablespoons instant
   minced onion
1 to 2 cloves garlic, crushed
2 6-ounce cans tomato
   paste

1 1-pound, 1-ounce can
   Italian tomatoes
2 teaspoons salt
¼ teaspoon pepper
1 tablespoon orégano
½ teaspoon basil
½ teaspoon thyme
½ teaspoon crushed red
   pepper
1 tablespoon snipped
   parsley
1 pound Mozzarella cheese
   slices

About 2 hours and 15 minutes before serving:

1. In large bowl, onto ½ cup warm water, sprinkle yeast; stir until dissolved. Mix in about 3 cups flour, 1 teaspoon salt, and ½ cup warm water; stir in ½ cup more warm water and remaining flour as in *photo a.*
2. On floured surface, knead dough until well blended.

Place in large greased bowl, turning to grease top. Cover with clean towel; set in warm place (80°F. to 85°F.) to rise until doubled in bulk — about 1 hour and 15 minutes.

3. Meanwhile, in hot olive oil, in large skillet, brown meat balls; stir in onion, garlic, tomato paste, tomatoes, 1½ cups water, 2 teaspoons salt, pepper, orégano, basil, thyme, red pepper, and parsley. Cook, covered, 1 hour, stirring occasionally.
4. Start heating oven to 450°F.
5. When dough has doubled, punch down; divide dough in half. Roll out each half on its own greased large cookie sheet to 13-inch round. Pinch up edges of each as in *photo b.* Brush edges with olive oil.
6. Pour tomato sauce over each round, spreading to edges; dot sauce with thin cheese slices as in *photo c.*
7. Bake about 25 minutes, or until edges and cheese are golden.
8. Cut each pizza into 8 wedges and serve piping hot with a fine Italian salad as in *photo d.* Makes 8 or 16 servings.

SUKIYAKI

½ cup bottled soy sauce
3 tablespoons granulated
 sugar
¾ cup canned chicken broth
About ½ head Chinese
 cabbage
About ½ pound fresh
 spinach
12 scallions
1 large onion
2 large mushrooms

1 or 2 canned bamboo
 shoots
About ⅓ can bean curd
 (optional)
1 can canned shirataki
 (optional)
1 pound very thinly sliced
 beef tenderloin or sirloin
2-inch square suet or 2
 tablespoons salad oil

About 1 hour before serving:
1.   Make this sauce: In pitcher combine soy sauce, sugar, and chicken broth; set aside.
2.   Cut enough Chinese cabbage into ½-inch diagonal slices, as in *photo a*, to measure 3 cups. Snip enough spinach to measure 3 cups. Slice scallions into 2-inch lengths.
3.   Cut onion in half lengthwise, then slice into ¼-inch slices. Slice mushrooms and bamboo shoots; cut bean curd into 8 small cubes.
4.   On platter or tray, attractively arrange all vegetables, shirataki, and meat, as in *photo b*. Place with suet and sauce on table set with hibachi and skillet, or electric skillet.
5.   Heat suet in skillet. With long fork, push from tray into skillet all but meat and spinach. Pour on sauce. Cook over high heat 8 minutes.
6.   Push spinach and meat onto vegetables; simmer 2 minutes, then push them down into sauce. Cook all 3 minutes.
7.   Serve as pictured, with rice and hot green tea. Makes 6 servings.
Note: Japanese food items are now available in many supermarkets.

RAINBOW MEAT LOAF

2 cups fresh bread crumbs
¼ cup minced onion
¼ cup minced celery
¼ cup minced green pepper
½ cup grated pared carrots
¼ cup snipped parsley
2 eggs, unbeaten

2 pounds chuck, ground
2 tablespoons prepared
 horse-radish
2½ teaspoons salt
1 teaspoon dry mustard
1 cup canned tomatoes

When it's convenient, prepare bread crumbs, onion, celery, green pepper, carrots, and parsley; set aside until needed.
About 1 hour before serving:
1.   Start heating oven to 400°F.
2.   In large bowl, with fork, beat eggs slightly. *Lightly* mix in chuck, then crumbs, onion, celery, green pepper, carrots, and parsley. (Meat will be juicier and more ten-

Sukiyaki

der if you handle it as little as possible.) Add horse-radish, salt, mustard, and tomatoes; combine lightly but well.

3. In bowl, shape meat mixture into oval loaf; transfer to shallow baking dish or broil-and-serve platter; smooth into shapely loaf.

4. Bake 50 minutes.

5. Serve from baking dish or platter, pouring off excess juices. Or, with 2 broad spatulas, lift loaf out of baking dish onto heated platter. Spoon some of juices over meat. (Nice chilled, then sliced, too.) Makes 8 servings.

Note: If you prefer a soft, moist interior, bake meat, as directed, in 9-by-5-by-3-inch loaf pan. Pour juices from pan after baking. Unmold meat loaf onto wire rack; then place, right side up, on heated platter. Or bake meat in 1½-quart ring mold for 45 minutes. Unmold, pouring off juices. Fill center with hot buttered or creamed vegetables.

HAMBURGER STROGANOFF IN TOMATO-RICE RING

1¼ cups uncooked regular white rice
1 teaspoon salt
½ cup chopped onion
¼ cup butter or margarine
1 pound chuck, ground
1 clove garlic, minced
2 tablespoons regular all-purpose flour
2 teaspoons salt
¼ teaspoon monosodium glutamate
¼ teaspoon paprika
¼ teaspoon pepper
1 pound fresh mushrooms, sliced
1 10½-ounce can condensed cream-of-chicken soup, undiluted
6 thin tomato slices
2 tablespoons butter or margarine
2 tablespoons snipped fresh dill
1 cup commercial sour cream

About 40 minutes before serving:

1. In large saucepan, with tightly fitting lid, combine rice with 2½ cups water and 1 teaspoon salt. Cook as package label directs.

2. Meanwhile, in large skillet, sauté onion in ¼ cup butter until golden. Stir in chuck, garlic, flour, 2 teaspoons salt, monosodium glutamate, paprika, pepper, and mushrooms; sauté 5 minutes. Add soup; simmer, uncovered, 10 minutes, stirring occasionally.

3. Meanwhile, line greased 5-cup ring mold with thin tomato slices as in *photo a.* With 2-tined fork, toss 2 tablespoons butter and snipped dill with hot rice. Gently pack rice mixture into ring mold. Let stand a minute or so. Then invert on heated serving plate; lift off mold as in *photo b.*

4. Stir sour cream into meat mixture as in *photo c,* until well combined. Spoon this Hamburger Stroganoff into Tomato-Rice Ring as in *photo d;* top with dill sprig. Serve with broccoli spears and head-lettuce wedges with Russian dressing, followed by chocolate cake. Makes 4 to 6 servings.

HONEYED PINEAPPLE-HAM LOAF

1 9-ounce can crushed pineapple
2 cans luncheon meat
2 tablespoons brown sugar
2 tablespoons liquid honey
Whole cloves

1. Start heating oven to 425°F.

2. Drain crushed pineapple. Remove luncheon meat from cans. Cut loaves into 4 slices each, not quite through to bottom. Place in greased 8-by-8-by-2-inch baking dish.

3. Mix crushed pineapple with brown sugar and honey. Spread this mixture between slices and over top of meat. Stud meat with whole cloves.

4. Bake 20 to 25 minutes. Makes 4 servings.

PINEAPPLE-HAM LOAF

3½ cups ground cooked or canned ham or luncheon meat*	¼ teaspoon pepper
	1 egg, slightly beaten
	¼ cup catchup
½ pound veal shoulder, ground	2 stalks celery, finely snipped
½ pound beef round, ground	¾ cup milk
	1 medium onion, minced
2 cups day-old bread crumbs	2 tablespoons snipped parsley
¼ teaspoon poultry seasoning	½ cup brown sugar, packed
½ teaspoon salt	4 canned pineapple slices

1. Start heating oven to 350°F.
2. In large bowl place ground ham, veal, and beef. Add crumbs, poultry seasoning, salt, pepper, egg, catchup, celery, milk, and onion. Add parsley. With 2-tined fork, lightly mix meat with other ingredients in bowl.
3. Sprinkle bottom of 9-by-9-by-2-inch baking dish with brown sugar. Arrange pineapple slices on top of sugar. With spoon and spatula, carefully press some of meat mixture around pineapple slices; then pat rest evenly on top.
4. Bake 1 hour.
5. When loaf is done, carefully pour off all drippings. To unmold, place platter or board on top of baking dish; invert so loaf rests, with pineapple side up, on platter or board; lift off baking dish. Spoon some of drippings over top. Makes 6 to 8 servings.
*When grinding ham or luncheon meat, use medium blade of food grinder.

ORANGE PORK CHOPS

4 center-cut loin pork chops, 1 inch thick	¼ teaspoon salt
	¼ teaspoon cinnamon
Salt and pepper	10 whole cloves
Paprika	2 teaspoons grated orange peel
2 to 4 tablespoons water	
5 tablespoons granulated sugar	½ cup orange juice
1½ teaspoons cornstarch	4 orange slices, halved

1. Trim some of fat from chops. In skillet, over low heat, heat a piece of fat; then remove.
2. Generously sprinkle both sides of chops with salt, pepper, and paprika. With tongs, arrange chops in skillet. Cook, over medium-high heat, until a rich golden brown on both sides—15 to 20 minutes. (As fat accumulates, tilt pan and spoon off fat.)

4. When chops are well browned, turn heat low. Add water. Cover skillet tightly. Cook chops 45 minutes to 1 hour, or until fork-tender and all pink has disappeared, turning them several times during cooking.

About 20 minutes before chops are done:
1. Make this Orange Glaze: In saucepan cook sugar, cornstarch, salt, cinnamon, cloves, and orange peel and juice, stirring, until thickened and clear. Add orange slices; cover pan; remove from heat.
2. Serve chops with a spoonful of Orange Glaze on each; garnish with orange slices. Nice served with hot corn bread, buttered peas, and coleslaw. Makes 4 servings.

STUFFED PORK CHOPS

6 rib pork chops, 1½-inches thick	1 10½-ounce can condensed beef broth, undiluted
3 cups fresh bread crumbs	1 teaspoon salt
1 cup diced canned ham	¼ teaspoon ground sage
⅛ teaspoon pepper	¼ teaspoon dried thyme
¼ teaspoon nutmeg	Salad oil
1 egg, beaten	6 canned pineapple slices, drained

About 2 hours before serving:
1. With paring knife, cut deep pocket in each chop.
2. Prepare bread crumbs; then combine crumbs with ham, pepper, and nutmeg. Combine egg with ½ cup beef broth; stir into crumb mixture.
3. Start heating oven to 450°F.
4. Rub chops, inside and out, and fat well with combined salt, sage, and thyme. Lightly pack chops with stuffing. (Wrap any extra stuffing in foil to bake with chops.)
5. Brush stuffed chops with salad oil. Place in shallow open foil-lined baking pan.
6. Bake, uncovered, 30 minutes. Reduce oven heat to 400°F. Remove chops from oven; drain off all fat. Mix ½ cup water with remaining beef broth; pour around chops. Cover pan with foil; bake 50 to 60 minutes, or until very tender.
7. Remove chops carefully to serving platter, overlapping slightly; place a pineapple slice between every two chops. Makes 6 servings.

LIVER AND BACON DE LUXE

¾ pound veal or calf liver, sliced ¼-inch thick	¼ cup minced onion
	⅓ cup white wine
½ pound bacon slices	Lemon juice
Seasoned flour	2 tablespoons snipped parsley
2 tablespoons butter or margarine	

1. Place liver slices on wax paper; sprinkle both sides with seasoned flour. (Never soak or scald liver.)

2. In 10-inch skillet, over low heat, fry bacon until crisp. Remove to paper towel; keep warm.
3. In skillet, heat ¼ cup bacon fat, or enough to cover bottom of skillet. Using tongs, place liver slices in skillet; cook quickly, turning once, until crisp brown on outside and delicate pink inside (medium done)—about 4 minutes in all. (Overcooking makes liver tough and hard.)
4. When liver is done, remove to heated platter. Pour all fat from skillet. Place skillet over low heat; add butter. Sauté onion in butter about 1 minute; add wine; bring to boiling. Cook 2 minutes, or until half original volume.
5. Sprinkle a few drops lemon juice over each slice of liver. Pour on wine sauce; garnish with parsley. Serve on heated platter with bacon slices. Makes 4 servings.
To vary: Omit onion and wine in step 4; heat butter slowly until golden brown. Pour over liver slices.

BLANQUETTE DE VEAU

2 pounds boned veal shoulder	1 tablespoon salt
4 whole cloves	¼ cup butter or margarine
1 small onion	15 small white onions (1 pound)
1 quart boiling water	½ pound small fresh mushrooms,
5 medium carrots, scraped, quartered	washed
1 bay leaf	2 tablespoons butter or margarine
⅛ teaspoon dried thyme	¼ cup regular all-purpose flour
2 sprigs parsley	2 egg yolks, unbeaten
½ cup thinly sliced celery	2 tablespoons lemon juice
4 peppercorns	Hot fluffy rice or mashed potatoes
	Snipped dill or parsley

About 2 hours and 30 minutes before serving:
1. Remove membrane and fat from veal; cut into 1¼-inch pieces. Simmer, in deep covered saucepan with clove-studded onion, boiling water, carrots, bay leaf, thyme, parsley, celery, peppercorns, and salt 1 hour, or until tender, as in *photo a.*
2. Drain stock from veal, reserving 3½ cups stock. Discard onion, bay leaf, peppercorns, and parsley. (Veal may be cooked day before, refrigerated, then reheated over very low heat.)
About 30 minutes before veal is done:
1. Melt ¼ cup butter in heavy skillet; add white onions; simmer, tightly covered, over low heat, 30 minutes, or until tender, as in *photo b.* Add to drained, cooked veal.
2. In same skillet, cook mushrooms in ½ cup veal stock, uncovered, 15 minutes. Add veal and onions.
3. Next, in same deep saucepan in which veal cooked, melt 2 tablespoons butter; stir in flour until smooth. Slowly stir in 3 cups reserved stock; cook, over medium heat, stirring, until thick and boiling.
4. In bowl, with wire whip, beat egg yolks with lemon juice; slowly stir in some of hot sauce as in *photo c;* stir egg-yolk mixture into hot stock. Pour this sauce over veal in skillet as in *photo d;* heat, but do not let it boil.
5. To serve, arrange ring of fluffy rice around veal as pictured; sprinkle with dill. Makes 6 servings.
Note: May be made day before, refrigerated, then reheated over very low heat.

Blanquette de Veau

CREAMED CHICKEN DE LUXE

⅓ cup butter or margarine
⅔ cup sliced fresh
  mushrooms
5 tablespoons regular
  all-purpose flour
½ teaspoon salt
Dash pepper

1⅓ cups chicken broth,
  canned, if desired
½ cup light cream
2 cups cut-up chunks
  cooked or canned
  chicken or turkey

1. In double-boiler top, over direct heat, melt butter; add mushrooms; sauté 5 minutes. Stir in flour, salt, and pepper until smooth.
2. Place over boiling water; slowly stir in broth and cream; cook, stirring, until thickened. Add chicken; heat well.
3. Serve on, with, or in: toast; waffles; baking-powder biscuits; split hot corn bread; buttered noodles, with croutons, almonds, or poppy seeds added; fluffy rice, tossed with snipped parsley or chutney; baked potatoes; mashed sweet potatoes; broiled pineapple slices; chow-mein noodles; toasted, split English muffins; pancakes; deviled-ham pinwheels; scrambled eggs or omelet; cooked broccoli or asparagus; patty shells; avocado halves; corn crisps. Makes 4 or 5 servings.

CREAMED CHICKEN AND HAM: Substitute cut-up, cooked ham for part of chicken.

CHICKEN À LA KING: Increase mushrooms to ¼ pound. Add 1 cut-up pimento and sherry to taste.

TURKETTI

1¼ cups 2-inch spaghetti
  pieces (not thin)
1½ to 2 cups cooked or
  canned turkey or
  chicken, in 1-inch
  chunks
½ cup diced cooked ham
  (optional)
¼ cup minced canned
  pimento
¼ cup minced green pepper

1 10½-ounce can
  condensed cream-of-
  mushroom soup,
  undiluted
½ cup turkey or canned
  chicken broth
⅛ teaspoon celery salt
⅛ teaspoon pepper
½ grated small onion
1½ cups grated natural or
  process sharp-Cheddar
  cheese (6 ounces)

Night before, or early on day:
1. Cook spaghetti until barely tender as label directs; drain.
2. Add turkey, ham, pimento, green pepper, soup, broth, celery salt, pepper, onion, and 1 cup grated cheese. Toss lightly; taste; add more seasonings, if desired.
3. Pour into 1½-quart casserole. Sprinkle with ½ cup grated cheese. Refrigerate.
About 1 hour before serving:
1. Start heating oven to 350°F.
2. Bake casserole, uncovered, 45 minutes, or until hot. Makes 4 servings.

Note: Twice the above recipe may be baked in a 3-quart casserole, uncovered, at 350°F., about 1 hour. Makes 8 servings.

CHICKEN TETRAZZINI

1 4½-pound roaster
  chicken, cut up
3 cups hot water
Salt
1 teaspoon onion salt
½ teaspoon celery salt
3 quarts water
½ pound spaghettini
6 tablespoons butter or
  margarine

½ pound fresh mushrooms,
  sliced
1 tablespoon lemon juice
2 tablespoons regular
  all-purpose flour
¼ teaspoon paprika
¼ teaspoon pepper
⅛ teaspoon nutmeg
1 cup heavy cream
⅔ cup grated Parmesan
  cheese

Day before:
1. In deep kettle, place chicken, hot water, 2 teaspoons salt, onion salt, and celery salt. Simmer, covered, until chicken is fork-tender — 1 to 1¼ hours. (As chicken cooks, add water if needed.)
2. Remove chicken to bowl (reserve broth); when cool enough to handle, remove meat from bones in big pieces; cut breast into thirds. Refrigerate chicken meat, covered, in bowl, at once.
3. Set aside 2½ cups chicken broth. To rest of broth in kettle add 3 quarts water and 2 tablespoons salt; bring to boil, then slowly add spaghettini (so water won't stop boiling); cook 6 minutes, or until tender, stirring occasionally.
4. Drain; place spaghettini in 12-by-8-by-2-inch baking dish.
5. Meanwhile, in medium skillet, heat 3 tablespoons butter. Add mushrooms; sprinkle with lemon juice and ½ teaspoon salt. Sauté mushrooms until soft, but not brown, stirring occasionally. Toss mushrooms and butter with cooked spaghettini; refrigerate, covered.
6. In saucepan, melt remaining butter; remove pan from heat and stir in flour, paprika, 1½ teaspoons salt, pepper, and nutmeg. Slowly stir in reserved broth (¼ cup sherry may replace ½ cup of this broth). Cook sauce, stirring, until thickened; add cream. Pour sauce over chicken; refrigerate, covered.
Next day, 1 hour before serving:
1. Start heating oven to 400°F.
2. With fork, stir up chicken and sauce, then pour as much of sauce as possible over spaghettini, tossing to mix well. Place rest of chicken-sauce mixture in center of spaghettini. Sprinkle with Parmesan cheese and more paprika.
3. Bake 25 minutes, or until hot.
4. Nice served with broiled candied apricots, garlicky mixed green salad, and toasted English muffins. Makes 8 servings.

PURPLE PLUM DUCKLINGS

2 5- to 6-pound ducklings,
    quartered
Onion salt
Garlic salt
4 oranges, halved crosswise
¼ cup butter or margarine
1 medium onion, chopped
1 17-ounce can purple plums

1 6-ounce can frozen lemonade
    concentrate, not reconstituted
⅓ cup chili sauce
¼ cup soy sauce
1 teaspoon Worcestershire
1 teaspoon ginger
2 teaspoons prepared mustard
2 drops Tabasco

1. Start heating oven to 350°F.
2. Sprinkle duckling quarters with onion and garlic salts; set each, on an orange half, on a trivet in a roasting pan. Roast 1½ hours.
3. Meanwhile, melt butter in large skillet; add onion; cook until tender. Set aside.
4. Empty can of plums with juice into food mill or strainer set over bowl as in *photo a*. Pit plums and purée them. Add purée to onion in skillet; blend in frozen lemonade, chili sauce, soy sauce, Worcestershire, ginger, mustard, and Tabasco; simmer 15 minutes.
5. After duckling quarters have roasted for 1½ hours, remove them, and oranges, and trivet from roasting pan. Drain off fat. Arrange duckling quarters and oranges, side by side, in roasting pan. Brush with plum sauce as in *photo b*. Return to oven for 15 minutes. Pour more sauce over them every 10 minutes, continuing to roast until quarters are tender, oranges and quarters are glazed.
6. Arrange duckling quarters and orange halves on large heated platter; pass rest of sauce. Makes 4 generous servings of 2 quarters each.

Purple Plum Ducklings

FISH CHOWDER

¼ pound salt pork
3 medium onions, sliced
5 medium potatoes, pared,
  sliced or diced
4 teaspoons salt
¼ teaspoon pepper
3 cups boiling water
1½ pounds fresh or thawed
  frozen haddock or cod
  fillets

1 quart milk, scalded
1 cup undiluted evaporated
  milk
3 tablespoons butter or
  margarine
Common crackers
Snipped parsley

1. Cut pork into ½-inch cubes; cook in large kettle until crispy brown, turning often; remove bits; reserve.
2. To hot pork fat in kettle, add onions; cook until just tender, stirring occasionally with a fork. Top with potatoes; sprinkle with salt and pepper; pour on boiling water.
3. Top with fish, cut into medium pieces. Cover; simmer 25 minutes, or until potatoes are just tender. Remove any skin from fish.
4. Add milk, evaporated milk, butter, and crisp pork bits; heat. Arrange split crackers on top; sprinkle with parsley. Makes 6 servings.

FILLETS VERONIQUE

3 tablespoons butter or
  margarine
1½ pounds fresh or thawed
  frozen fish fillets*
1 teaspoon salt
⅛ to ¼ teaspoon pepper
1 clove garlic (optional)
1 medium onion, minced

2 shallots, minced (optional)
1 teaspoon lemon juice
2 teaspoons regular
  all-purpose flour
¼ cup light cream
2 cups fresh green seedless
  grapes, halved

1. In 10-inch skillet, with tight-fitting lid, melt 2 tablespoons butter; arrange fillets in skillet; sprinkle with salt and pepper. Stick toothpick into garlic; lay on top of fish. Sprinkle with onion and shallots. Mix ¼ cup water (or ¼ cup white wine) with lemon juice; pour around fillets.
2. Tear or cut circle of wax paper to fit skillet; tear small hole in center as in *photo a*. (By using wax paper circle, you can cook fillets without drowning them in liquid. Hole in wax paper allows steam to escape.) Place paper circle on fish. Bring to boil; cover; cook over high heat 5 to 10 minutes, or until easily flaked with fork, *but still moist*. Remove cover, paper, and garlic.
3. Mix 1 tablespoon butter with flour as in *photo b*. Pour cream around fish; stir butter-flour mixture into cream, moving skillet in a circular motion to combine and thicken sauce; spoon over fish.
4. Sprinkle grapes around edge of skillet as in *photo c*. Serve fish immediately from skillet. Nice with tiny boiled new potatoes, rolled in snipped dill or parsley, or rice. Makes 4 to 6 servings.
*Fillets of flounder, fluke, yellowtail, sole, ocean perch, haddock, cod, sea bass, and pompano poach well.

FILLETS THERMIDOR

3 pounds fresh or thawed
  frozen fish fillets
2¼ cups milk
1½ teaspoons salt
⅛ teaspoon pepper
½ pound process sharp-
  Cheddar cheese

½ cup butter or margarine
½ cup regular all-purpose
  flour
½ cup lemon juice or sherry
Paprika (optional)

1. Start heating oven to 350°F.
2. Roll up each fillet (split lengthwise if 8 inches or longer); stand on end in shallow 2-quart casserole. Pour milk over fish; sprinkle with salt and pepper.
3. Bake, uncovered, about 30 minutes, or until easily flaked with fork, *but still moist*. (Thick fillets may take 40 minutes.)
4. Meanwhile, coarsely grate cheese.
5. When fish is done, remove from oven; turn oven up to "Broil." Spoon some of milk from fish into large measuring cup, to avoid spilling, then carefully pour in rest of milk.
6. Melt butter in double boiler, stir in flour; then slowly stir in milk drained from fish. Cook, stirring, until thickened. Add cheese; stir until melted. Add

Rice-Crusted Tuna Pie

lemon juice. Pour over baked fish; sprinkle with paprika, if desired. Brown quickly under broiler. Makes 8 servings.

FOR 4: Use 1½ pounds fillets. Reduce milk to 1½ cups, salt to 1 teaspoon. Use speck pepper, ¼ pound cheese, 3 tablespoons each butter, flour, and sherry or lemon juice. Bake in 10-by-6-by-2-inch baking dish.

RICE-CRUSTED TUNA PIE

2⅔ cups cooked rice	1¾ cups finely grated
1½ tablespoons melted	Swiss cheese
butter or margarine	¾ cup scalded milk
1 egg, slightly beaten	2 eggs, unbeaten
2 tomatoes	¼ teaspoon salt
French dressing	⅛ teaspoon pepper
1 6½- or 7-ounce can tuna	⅛ teaspoon nutmeg
	Snipped scallions

1. In bowl, combine rice, melted butter, and beaten egg. Turn into 9-inch pie plate. Using back of tablespoon, press mixture firmly against side and bottom of pie plate as in *photo a,* being careful to heap rice high on rim.

2. Cut each tomato into six wedges; let stand in bowl in French dressing to cover.

3. Start heating oven to 400°F.

4. In bowl, flake tuna. Sprinkle ¾ cup grated cheese over rice crust, then top with scant half of tuna; then sprinkle with rest of cheese, piling it high in center.

5. Combine milk, 2 eggs, salt, pepper, and nutmeg until well blended. Pour over cheese in rice-lined pie plate. Sprinkle remaining tuna on top.

6. Bake 25 minutes. Place tomato wedges around inner edge as in *photo b.* Bake 10 minutes longer, or until silver knife inserted in center comes out clean as in *photo c.*

7. Sprinkle scallions around tomatoes. Serve pie cut in wedges. Makes 8 servings.

SHRIMP CREOLE

3 pounds raw shrimp in shells
1½ seeded green peppers
3 or 4 cloves garlic, minced
3 large onions
6 tablespoons salad oil
4 cups hot seasoned cooked rice
1 tablespoon salt
⅛ teaspoon pepper
½ teaspoon dried rosemary
½ teaspoon paprika
6 dashes Tabasco
2 1-pound 13-ounce cans tomatoes
  (about 6 cups)
1 cup snipped parsley

Early on day:
Shell shrimp; cut out vein along outside curve as in *photo a*. Rinse, drain, then refrigerate shrimp.

About 45 minutes before serving:
1.   Snip green peppers into ½-inch pieces. Chop onions by first making parallel cuts almost to base of each, next repeating these cuts across first ones, then turning onion on side and slicing off small bits as in *photo b*.
2.   Place all vegetables in automatic skillet (or large regular skillet); add oil and sauté at 375°F. (medium heat) until tender.
3.   Meanwhile, start cooking rice as label directs.
4.   To tender vegetables add salt, pepper, rosemary, paprika, Tabasco, and tomatoes. Cook at 225°F. (medium low heat) 15 minutes, stirring occasionally. Add shrimp and cook just until shrimp turn pink as in *photo c*. Turn automatic skillet to 150°F.
5.   Mound shrimp mixture in center of automatic skillet. Add parsley to cooked rice; spoon ring of rice around shrimp. (Or transfer shrimp from regular skillet to platter; surround with rice.) Makes 8 to 10 servings.
FOR 4: Halve all ingredients; prepare as above.

Shrimp Cre

SCALLOPED OYSTERS

2 cups coarse toast crumbs
¼ cup melted butter or
   margarine
2 dozen shucked raw
   oysters
¼ cup oyster liquid
½ teaspoon salt

¼ teaspoon pepper
2 tablespoons light cream
1 teaspoon Worcestershire
Dash cayenne pepper
2 tablespoons sherry or
   light cream

1. To make toast crumbs, toast 4 white-bread slices. With kitchen scissors, snip into pieces.
2. Start heating oven to 425°F.
3. Combine crumbs and butter; use one third of mixture to cover bottom of greased 12-by-8-by-2-inch baking dish.
4. Drain oysters, reserving liquid. Arrange half of oysters on crumbs. Combine ¼ cup oyster liquid with salt, pepper, cream, Worcestershire, cayenne, and sherry. Spoon half of this sauce over oysters.
5. Sprinkle with one third of crumbs; top with rest of oysters, then top with rest of sauce. Sprinkle with remaining crumbs.
6. Bake, uncovered, 30 minutes. Makes 4 servings.

CHAFING-DISH SEAFOOD NEWBURG

2 quarts water
2 teaspoons salt
1 tablespoon shrimp spice
1 pound sea scallops
1 pound deveined, shelled
   raw shrimp
6 round buns
Melted butter or margarine

6 tablespoons butter or
   margarine
2 tablespoons flour
⅛ teaspoon nutmeg
Dash paprika
1 teaspoon salt
3 tablespoons sherry
2 cups light cream
3 egg yolks, slightly beaten

About 30 minutes before serving:
1. Bring water to boil with 2 teaspoons salt and shrimp spice, tied in cheesecloth bag.
2. Cut scallops in half; drop into boiling water. When water boils again, add shrimp. Cook, covered, 3 minutes; drain and set aside.
3. Start heating oven to 400°F.
4. Make mock patty shells: With fork, scrape out center top of buns; place buns on ungreased cookie sheet. Brush with melted butter.
5. Bake about 10 minutes, or until toasty. Keep warm while cooking Newburg in chafing dish.
6. Heat water in hot-water pan of chafing dish until it simmers. Melt 6 tablespoons butter in chafing dish; stir in flour, nutmeg, paprika, and 1 teaspoon salt until smooth. Stir in sherry, then sea food. Cook mixture until sea food is heated through.
7. Combine cream and egg yolks; slowly pour into chafing dish, stirring constantly. Continue stirring gently until sauce becomes thickened and smooth.

8. Spoon into "patty shells." Serve with green beans mixed with peas, and celery and carrot sticks. Makes 6 servings.
Note: Seafood Newburg may be made in double boiler if more convenient.

CHEESE-AND-ONION CASSEROLE

1 cup minced onions
¼ cup shortening or
   salad oil
2 cups grated process
   sharp-Cheddar cheese
   (½ pound)
½ teaspoon salt

⅛ teaspoon pepper
½ teaspoon dry mustard
7 day-old white-bread slices
2 tablespoons butter or
   margarine
2 cups milk

1. Start heating oven to 350°F.
2. Sauté onions in shortening until golden. Add cheese, salt, pepper, and mustard; cook, stirring, until cheese is melted; remove from heat.
3. Spread bread slices with butter. In 1½-quart casserole, alternate layers of bread and cheese. Pour on milk.
4. Bake, uncovered, 1 hour. Makes 4 servings.

CHEESE SOUFFLÉ FOR SIX

1½ cups milk, or ¾ cup
   evaporated milk plus
   ¾ cup water
¼ cup butter or margarine
¼ cup regular all-purpose
   flour

1 teaspoon salt
Speck cayenne pepper
½ pound process sharp-
   Cheddar cheese
6 eggs, separated

1. Start heating oven to 300°F.
2. In saucepan, heat, but do not scald, milk.
3. In double boiler melt butter. Stir in flour, then heated milk, salt, and cayenne; cook, stirring, until thickened and smooth. Thinly slice cheese right into sauce. Stir until cheese melts completely and sauce is velvety smooth; remove from heat.
4. With fork, beat egg yolks until well blended. Stir in a little of cheese sauce. Slowly stir this mixture back into rest of cheese sauce.
5. With mixer or hand beater, beat egg whites until stiff but not dry. Slowly pour in cheese sauce, folding until no large areas of egg white remain.
6. Pour mixture into *ungreased* 2-quart casserole up to within ¼ inch of top. (Bake any extra mixture in small *ungreased* casserole.)
7. To form crown, with teaspoon, make shallow path in soufflé mixture about 1 inch in from edge of casserole all the way around.
8. Bake, uncovered, 1¼ hours; *don't open oven while soufflé is baking.*
9. Serve at once. Sautéed tomato halves and crisp bacon are nice accompaniments. Makes 6 servings.

CHEESE-AND-RICE SOUFFLÉ

1 cup cooked rice	½ pound process sharp-
2 tablespoons butter or	Cheddar cheese
margarine	4 eggs, separated
3 tablespoons flour	½ teaspoon salt
¾ cup milk	Dash cayenne pepper

1. Cook rice as package label directs.
2. Start heating oven to 325°F.
3. In double boiler melt butter; stir in flour until smooth, then milk. Cook, stirring, until thickened. Slice cheese thinly, right into sauce; cook, stirring occasionally, until cheese is melted and sauce thickened.
4. To egg yolks, add salt and cayenne; beat with fork; slowly add to cheese sauce, stirring constantly. Remove sauce from heat; fold in rice.
5. With mixer or hand beater, beat egg whites until stiff but not dry. Gently fold in cheese-rice mixture. Turn into greased 1½-quart casserole. To form crown, with spoon, make shallow path in cheese-rice mixture about 1 inch in from edge all the way around.
6. Bake, uncovered, 40 minutes. Serve at once. Makes 5 servings.

VEGETABLE STYLE: Just before folding in egg whites, add 1 cup chopped, cooked broccoli or cooked green beans.

Hot soufflés are extremely temperamental! They don't like to wait for people, so serve them the minute they are done, if possible. However, if dinner is delayed a bit, you can leave a soufflé in the oven, with heat turned down to 250°F., but only for a few minutes.

SWISS PIE

1 quart toasted ½-inch	2 cups grated natural Swiss
bread squares	cheese (½ pound)
2 tomatoes, sliced	2 eggs, unbeaten
Salt	½ teaspoon paprika
Pepper	½ teaspoon dry mustard
	1½ cups milk

1. Start heating oven to 350°F.
2. Place bread squares in 9-inch pie plate. Top with tomato slices; sprinkle with salt, pepper, and cheese.
3. With fork, mix eggs with ¾ teaspoon salt, paprika, mustard, ⅛ teaspoon pepper, and milk. Pour over cheese mixture.
4. Bake 40 minutes, or until puffy and brown. Makes 4 servings.

BAKED EGGS IN CHEESE SAUCE

3 tablespoons butter or	1 teaspoon prepared
margarine	mustard
3 tablespoons regular	1½ cups milk
all-purpose flour	1 cup grated process
Speck pepper	Cheddar cheese
¾ teaspoon salt	(¼ pound)
	6 eggs, unbeaten

1. Melt butter in double boiler; stir in flour, pepper, salt, mustard, then milk. Cook, stirring, until thickened and smooth. Add cheese; stir until melted.
2. Start heating oven to 325°F.
3. Cover bottom of greased 10-by-6-by-2-inch baking dish with half of sauce. Carefully break eggs, one by one, into cup; slide onto sauce, side by side; cover with rest of sauce.
4. Bake, uncovered, about 20 to 25 minutes, or until eggs are done as you like.
5. Serve from baking dish, or on toast. Makes 6 servings.

BAKED MACARONI AND CHEESE

½ pound macaroni, in	¼ teaspoon dry mustard
2½-inch pieces, or	¾ teaspoon salt
elbow macaroni (about	Speck pepper
2 cups)	2 cups milk
1 small onion, minced	½ pound process Cheddar
(about 4 teaspoons)	cheese, medium grated
2 tablespoons butter or	or sliced
margarine	¾ cup fresh bread crumbs
1 tablespoon regular	4 teaspoons melted butter
all-purpose flour	or margarine

1. Cook macaroni as label directs.
2. Start heating oven to 400°F.
3. Place minced onion and butter in double boiler. When butter is melted, stir in flour, mustard, salt, and pepper. Slowly stir in milk; cook, stirring often, until smooth and hot.
4. Add about three fourths of cheese (slice right into sauce, if desired); stir until cheese is melted.
5. When macaroni is tender, drain into colander; turn into greased 1½-quart casserole. Pour cheese sauce over macaroni, tossing lightly with fork to coat all macaroni with sauce. Top with rest of cheese.
6. Toss bread crumbs with melted butter; sprinkle over cheese.
7. Bake, uncovered, 20 minutes. Nice with crisp bacon. Makes 4 main-dish servings, or 6 servings if substituted for potatoes.

FOR 2: Use following ingredients: ⅓ pound cheese, 1⅓ cups macaroni, 1 tablespoon onion, 4 teaspoons butter or margarine, 2 teaspoons flour, ¼ teaspoon dry mustard, ½ teaspoon salt, speck pepper, 1⅓ cups milk, ½ cup bread crumbs, and 1 tablespoon melted butter or margarine. Bake in a 1-quart casserole.

BAKED MACARONI WITH GREEN BEANS: With cheese, in step 5, add 2 cups cooked green beans.

BAKED-TOMATO MACARONI: Arrange 2 or 3 sliced, peeled tomatoes in layers with macaroni and sauce.

BAKED MACARONI WITH HAM: With sauce, in step 5, add ½ to 1½ cups slivered, cooked ham, tongue, chicken, or luncheon meat. (If using tongue or ham, reduce salt to ½ teaspoon.)

EGGS BENEDICT

2 egg yolks, unbeaten
Dash cayenne pepper
Butter or margarine
1 tablespoon lemon juice

2 English muffins
4 slices cooked or boiled ham
4 eggs, unbeaten
Water cress

1. Make Hollandaise: With mixer or hand beater, beat egg yolks until thick and lemon-colored; add cayenne. Slowly add ¼ cup melted butter, about 1 teaspoon at a time as in *photo a*, beating constantly. Blend ¼ cup melted butter with lemon juice; add to egg-yolk mixture, 2 teaspoons at a time, beating constantly. Keep warm.

2. Preheat broiler 10 minutes, or as manufacturer directs. With fork, deeply prick each muffin midway around side as in *photo b*, then gently pull halves apart. Spread muffins with butter; place on cookie sheet (or broiler pan), with ham slices alongside. Broil until muffin halves are toasted, ham is curled. Then, on platter, place a ham slice on each muffin half. Keep warm.

3. Fill buttered 10-inch skillet with enough water to cover eggs by 1 inch. Bring to boil; lower heat so water just simmers. Break egg into cup; lower cup close to surface of water; quickly slip egg into water as in *photo c*. Repeat, placing 4 eggs side by side.

4. Cover skillet; while keeping water hot, not simmering, cook eggs until whites are solid, yolks of desired firmness—3 to 5 minutes.

5. Now slip slotted spoon under each egg, lift out of water, tilt slightly against side of skillet to drain well, then set on ham-topped muffins. Spoon on Hollandaise sauce as in *photo d*; garnish with water cress. Makes 4 servings.

LASAGNA

¾ pound chuck, ground
¼ pound boned pork shoulder, ground
4 eggs, unbeaten
About 1 cup grated Romano or Parmesan cheese
¾ cup packaged dried bread crumbs
7 tablespoons snipped parsley
Salt
1 pound sweet or hot Italian sausages
2 cloves garlic

1 6-ounce can tomato paste (⅔ cup)
3 1-pound 13-ounce cans Italian-style tomatoes (10 cups)
½ teaspoon fennel seeds
1 pound lasagna noodles
1 teaspoon dried basil
3 pounds riccota or cottage cheese
½ to 1 teaspoon freshly ground pepper
1 pound Mozzarella or natural Swiss cheese, thinly sliced

Day before:
1. Mix chuck, pork, 2 eggs, 2 tablespoons grated Romano cheese,

crumbs, 1 tablespoon snipped parsley, and 1 teaspoon salt. Divide mixture in half. Shape half into 10 large meat balls, rest into tiny balls—about 4 dozen.

2. In Dutch oven, brown sausages with 1 clove garlic until some fat collects. Add meat balls; brown. Remove sausages and meat balls.

3. To fat remaining in Dutch oven, add tomato paste; cook over low heat a few minutes. Add tomatoes, 1 tablespoon salt, and fennel seeds; simmer, uncovered, stirring frequently, about 1 hour, or until very thick. Add sausages, meat balls, and 2½ cups water; cook slowly, uncovered, about 2 hours.

4. Remove sausages and large meat balls. Cool; refrigerate all.

About 2 hours before serving:

1. Cook lasagna noodles as label directs, until they seem tender—and not hard in center. (Taste a strand now and then to be sure and not overcook them.) Quickly drain noodles and hang them over side of colander for easier handling.

2. Meanwhile, heat sauce over low heat until it bubbles. Add 2 tablespoons snipped parsley, 1 minced clove garlic, and basil. Remove 1 cup of sauce, add it to large meat balls and sausages; set it aside.

3. Blend well ricotta, 2 eggs, ¼ cup snipped parsley, 1 tablespoon salt, and pepper.

4. Start heating oven to 400°F.

5. In shallow open 14-by-10-by-2-inch pan, spread one fourth of sauce. Lay about one third of noodles, one at a time, over sauce in pan, until bottom is entirely covered with noodles. Spread half of ricotta mixture over noodle layer. Sprinkle this with about ⅓ cup grated Romano cheese; dot with ⅓ pound Mozzarella, in thin slices.

6. Repeat layers of sauce, noodles, ricotta mixture, and cheeses; then add another one fourth of sauce and remaining noodles. Sprinkle top layer of noodles with remaining grated cheese; spread rest of sauce over entire surface, and dot with remaining Mozzarella.

7. Bake 1 hour, then remove from oven and let stand on top of range 15 to 30 minutes so it will cut easily. Meanwhile, slowly reheat sausages and large meat balls in sauce.

8. When serving lasagna, pass sausages and large meat balls in sauce. Nice with tossed green salad with anchovies and pimento, crisp French bread, plus fresh fruit, or sherbet, or fruited wine jelly for dessert. Makes 10 to 12 servings.

To vary: For sauce ingredients, substitute 6 10¼-ounce cans Marinara sauce plus 2 cans water and 1 teaspoon salt. Cook this sauce with sausages and meat balls for a total of 30 minutes, instead of the 3 hours which sauce above requires. Layer and bake as directed.

ZITI AL FORNO: Substitute 1 pound ziti for lasagna noodles. Layer and bake as above.

Cookies

DOUBLE CHOCOLATE-WALNUT DROPS

1½ cups sifted regular all-purpose flour	1 egg, unbeaten
1 teaspoon double-acting baking powder	2 tablespoons milk
¾ teaspoon salt	1 teaspoon vanilla extract
¾ cup soft shortening	½ cup semisweet-chocolate pieces
¾ cup granulated sugar	¾ cup chopped walnuts
1 square unsweetened chocolate, melted	Walnut halves

1. Start heating oven to 350°F.
2. Sift flour with baking powder and salt.
3. In large bowl, with mixer at medium speed (or with spoon), mix shortening with sugar, then with melted chocolate and egg, until light and fluffy.
4. At low speed, mix in milk, then flour mixture; add vanilla, chocolate pieces, and chopped walnuts.
5. Drop, by heaping teaspoonfuls, about 1 inch apart, onto greased cookie sheets; press walnut half into top of some.
6. Bake 15 to 18 minutes.
7. Cool on wire rack. Makes about 4 dozen.

REFRIGERATOR COOKIES

1½ cups sifted regular all-purpose flour	1 egg, unbeaten
½ teaspoon baking soda	2 or 3 teaspoons vanilla extract, or ½ teaspoon almond extract
¾ teaspoon salt	
½ cup soft shortening	½ cup coarsely chopped nuts (optional)
1 cup granulated sugar, or ½ cup each granulated sugar and brown sugar, packed	

1. Sift flour with baking soda and salt.
2. Mix shortening with sugar, egg, and vanilla until very light and fluffy. Gradually mix in flour and nuts.
3. Turn dough onto large piece of wax paper or foil. Shape into roll 1½ inches in diameter; then wrap in wax paper, foil, or saran. Refrigerate several hours, overnight, or for a week, if desired.

At baking time:

1. Start heating oven to 375°F.
2. With sharp thin knife, dipped into hot water and wiped dry, slice off of roll as many ⅛- to ¼-inch thick slices as desired. (Return rest of roll, wrapped, to refrigerator.) Place on ungreased cookie sheet.

3. Bake 10 minutes, or until done.

4. Cool on wire rack; store in tightly-covered container. Makes about 5 dozen.

ORANGE: Add 1 tablespoon grated orange peel to egg mixture; substitute orange juice for vanilla.

SPICE-NUT: Sift ½ teaspoon cinnamon and ¼ teaspoon nutmeg with flour mixture.

COCONUT: Increase shortening to ¾ cup. Use granulated-brown sugar combination. Add 2 cups flaked coconut.

CHOCOLATE: Add 3 squares melted unsweetened chocolate to egg mixture before adding flour. Decrease vanilla to 1 teaspoon.

DATE: Add ½ cup chopped, pitted dates to flour mixture.

SUSAN'S BROWNIES

¾ cup sifted cake flour
½ teaspoon double-acting
   baking powder
¾ teaspoon salt
1 cup granulated sugar
½ cup soft shortening

2 eggs, unbeaten
1 teaspoon vanilla extract
2 to 2½ squares
   unsweetened chocolate,
   melted
1 cup chopped nuts

1. Start heating oven to 350°F.
2. Sift flour with baking powder and salt.
3. Gradually add sugar to shortening, mixing until *very light and fluffy*. Add eggs and vanilla; mix until smooth. Mix in chocolate, then flour mixture and nuts. (If desired, reserve half of nuts to sprinkle on top of batter before baking.) Turn into greased 8-by-8-by-2-inch pan.
4. Bake 30 to 35 minutes, or until done.
5. Cool slightly; cut into 16 squares or bars; dust with confectioners' sugar, if desired. Store in pan.

TOFFEE BARS

½ cup soft butter or
   margarine
¼ cup granulated sugar
¼ cup brown sugar, packed
¼ teaspoon salt
1 teaspoon vanilla extract
1 egg, unbeaten

½ cup sifted regular all-
   purpose flour
½ cup uncooked rolled oats
1 6-ounce package semi-
   sweet-chocolate pieces
   (1 cup)
¼ cup flaked coconut
¼ cup chopped walnuts

1. Start heating oven to 350°F.
2. Mix butter, granulated and brown sugars, salt, vanilla, and egg until *very light and fluffy*. Mix in flour and rolled oats; blend well. Spread in greased 11-by-7-by-1½-inch baking pan.
3. Bake 30 minutes, or until done.
4. Cool 10 minutes. Meanwhile, melt chocolate pieces over hot, *not boiling*, water; stir until smooth. Spread over baked layer; sprinkle half with coconut, other half with nuts. Cool in pan. Cut into 24 bars.

Cakes

YELLOW LAYER CAKE

2 eggs, unbeaten
1 cup milk
½ cup soft shortening*
2½ cups sifted cake flour
1½ cups granulated sugar

3 teaspoons double-acting
   baking powder
1 teaspoon salt
1 teaspoon vanilla extract
Apricot jam
Fluffy Frosting, below

About 2 hours ahead:

1. Set out eggs, milk, and shortening to come to room temperature—about 1 hour.
2. Start heating oven to 375°F.
3. Into large bowl sift flour with sugar, baking powder, and salt. Drop in shortening, then pour in ⅔ cup milk and vanilla.
4. With mixer at medium speed, beat 2 minutes. Or beat with spoon 300 sweeping round-the-bowl strokes, 2 minutes, rotating bowl and scraping it often.
5. Add ⅓ cup milk and eggs; beat with mixer at medium speed 2 minutes, or with spoon 300 strokes—2 minutes. Pour batter into 2 greased and floured 8-inch layer-cake pans, dividing equally. (Or line pans with wax paper; grease paper.)
6. Bake 25 to 30 minutes, or until tops of cakes spring back when gently pressed in center with finger.
7. Cool layers in pans on wire racks 10 to 15 minutes. With spatula, loosen each layer around sides, place rack on top, invert cake on it and lift off pan. (Remove wax paper.) Turn cakes right side up to cool.
8. Fill with apricot jam, frost with Fluffy Frosting.

*Use any shortening that comes in a 1-pound or 3-pound can.

FLUFFY FROSTING: In small saucepan combine 1¼ cups granulated sugar, ⅛ teaspoon cream of tartar, 6 tablespoons water, and pinch salt, stir over low heat until sugar dissolves. Cook, without stirring, to 260°F. on candy thermometer, or until mixture dropped in cold water forms a hard ball. Set syrup aside. With mixer at high speed, beat 3 egg whites until they form moist peaks when beater is raised. Now add syrup gradually, beating constantly; add 1 teaspoon vanilla extract. Continue beating until mixture forms stiff peaks when beater is raised and is thick enough to spread.

To vary: Sprinkle chopped nuts or shaved unsweetened chocolate in border around top edge of frosted cake. *Note:* Cake may be baked in greased, floured 14-by-10-by-2-inch pan; cool, then sprinkle with confectioners' sugar; cut into diamonds.

THREE-LAYER FUDGE CAKE

2 cups sifted cake flour	3 squares unsweetened
2 cups granulated sugar	chocolate, melted
1 teaspoon salt	1¼ cups milk
1½ teaspoons baking soda	1 teaspoon vanilla extract
¾ teaspoon double-acting	3 medium eggs, unbeaten
baking powder	Mocha Butter Cream, below
½ cup soft shortening*	

1. Start heating oven to 350°F.
2. In large bowl sift flour with sugar, salt, baking soda, and baking powder. Drop in shortening; pour in chocolate, ¾ cup milk, and vanilla.
3. With mixer at medium speed, beat 2 minutes, scraping bowl and beaters as needed. Or with spoon beat 300 sweeping round-the-bowl strokes. Add ½ cup milk and eggs; beat 2 minutes as before. Turn into 3 8-inch layer-cake pans that have been greased and lined with wax paper on bottoms only.
4. Bake 35 to 40 minutes, or until cake tester, inserted in center, comes out clean.
5. Cool in pans on wire racks 10 to 15 minutes; then loosen cakes with spatula, remove and cool.
6. Fill and frost with Mocha Butter Cream.
*Use any shortening that comes in 1-pound or 3-pound can.

MOCHA BUTTER CREAM: With mixer at medium speed (or with spoon), thoroughly mix ⅔ cup butter, margarine, or shortening with ¼ teaspoon salt, and 1 1-pound package confectioners' sugar sifted with ½ cup cocoa until light and fluffy. Add another 1-pound package confectioners' sugar sifted with ½ cup cocoa alternately with ⅔ cup hot coffee, beating until very smooth and of spreading consistency; add 1 teaspoon vanilla.

CHOCOLATE ROLL

4 eggs, unbeaten	1 teaspoon vanilla extract
½ cup sifted cake flour	2 tablespoons granulated
½ teaspoon double-acting	sugar
baking powder	¼ teaspoon baking soda
¼ teaspoon salt	3 tablespoons cold water
2 squares unsweetened	Confectioners' sugar
chocolate	1 cup heavy cream
¾ cup granulated sugar	¼ teaspoon almond extract

1. Set out eggs to come to room temperature—about 1 hour.
2. Start heating oven to 375°F.
3. Onto wax paper sift flour with baking powder and salt. Melt chocolate.
4. Break eggs into large bowl; sift ¾ cup sugar over them. With mixer at high speed (or with hand beater), beat until *very light and fluffy.*
5. With rubber spatula or spoon, fold flour mixture and vanilla, all at once, into egg mixture. To melted chocolate, add 2 tablespoons sugar, baking soda, and water; stir until thick and light; fold into batter. Turn into 15½-by-10½-by-1-inch jelly-roll pan that has been greased, then lined in bottom with wax paper.
6. Bake 15 to 20 minutes, or just until cake springs back when lightly touched in center.
7. Meanwhile, place clean towel on flat surface; over it sift thick layer of confectioners' sugar. When cake is done, with spatula, loosen it from sides of pan, invert onto towel. Lift off pan; carefully remove wax paper. With very sharp knife, cut crisp edges from cake, to make rolling easier. Cool exactly 5 minutes.
8. Now roll up cake in towel from narrow end, rolling towel in it (this prevents cake from sticking). Gently lift rolled cake to wire rack to complete cooling—about 1 hour. (If cake is warm, whipped-cream filling will melt.)

Just before serving:
1. Whip cream with almond extract. Carefully unroll cake so it will be on towel. Quickly spread cream filling to within 1 inch of edges. Start rolling up cake from narrow end by folding edge of cake over, then tucking it under; continue rolling cake, lifting towel higher and higher with one hand as you guide roll with other hand. Finish with open end of cake on underside.
2. Cut into crosswise slices; serve plain, or top with vanilla or coffee ice cream. Makes 8 to 10 servings.

CHOCOLATE-CRUNCH ROLL: Omit 1 cup heavy cream and almond extract. In double boiler, over hot, *not boiling,* water, melt ½ cup semisweet-chocolate pieces with 2 tablespoons white corn syrup and 2 tablespoons butter or margarine. Whip ¾ cup heavy cream with 1 teaspoon instant coffee powder until stiff; fold in 1 cup very finely-crushed peanut brittle. Use as filling for cake roll; spread chocolate mixture on top.

WALNUT CAKE

1 cup soft shortening*	1½ teaspoons salt
¾ cup milk	2 teaspoons vanilla extract
4 eggs, unbeaten	1 cup very finely chopped
3 cups sifted cake flour	walnuts
1¾ cups granulated sugar	Glaze, below
2 teaspoons double-acting	
baking powder	

1. Set out shortening, milk, and eggs to come to room temperature—about 1 hour.
2. Start heating oven to 375°F.
3. Into large bowl sift flour with sugar, baking powder, and salt. Drop in shortening and 2 eggs; pour in milk and vanilla.
4. With mixer at medium speed, beat 2 minutes, scraping bowl and beaters as needed (or beat 300 sweeping round-the-bowl strokes with a spoon). Add 2 eggs; repeat, beating 2 minutes as before. Fold in nuts. Turn

batter into greased 9-inch tube pan that has been lined in bottom with wax paper.

5. Bake 1 hour, or until cake tester, inserted in center, comes out clean.

6. Set pan on wire rack; cool 10 to 15 minutes. Loosen cake with spatula, remove, and cool.

7. Meanwhile, make glaze. When cake has cooled, decorate with walnut halves and candied citron or pineapple as pictured, or use well-drained canned pineapple tidbits. Then drizzle on glaze, letting some run down sides. This cake freezes well.

*Use any shortening that comes in 1-pound or 3-pound can.

GLAZE: In small saucepan combine 2 tablespoons light corn syrup and 2 tablespoons butter or margarine. Boil 3 minutes, *no longer*.

SPONGECAKE

5 eggs, separated	4½ teaspoons lemon juice
1 cup sifted granulated sugar	2 tablespoons water
1½ teaspoons grated lemon peel	1 cup sifted cake flour
	¼ teaspoon salt
	¼ teaspoon cream of tartar

1. Set out eggs to come to room temperature—about 1 hour.

2. Start heating oven to 350°F.

3. In small bowl, with mixer at high speed (or with hand beater), beat egg yolks until blended. Gradually add ½ cup sugar, beating constantly.

4. Combine lemon peel and juice with water; gradually add to egg-yolk mixture, beating until light and fluffy.

Walnut Cake

5. With rubber spatula, gently fold flour into egg yolks until they are completely blended.

6. In large bowl, with mixer at high speed (or with hand beater), beat egg whites with salt until foamy. Add cream of tartar; continue beating until moist peaks form when beater is raised. Beat in ½ cup sugar, 2 tablespoons at a time.

7. Turn egg-yolk mixture onto beaten whites. With rubber spatula or spoon, gently fold yolks into whites until so thoroughly blended there are no streaks of yolks or whites.

8. Pour mixture into ungreased 9-inch tube pan, turning pan slowly as you pour. To remove large air bubbles, cut through batter with spatula, in shape of square, lifting spatula out of batter and inserting it again at each corner of square.

9. Bake cake 40 to 45 minutes, or until cake springs back when lightly touched in center.

10. Cool cake, inverted in pan, about 1 hour, or until cold. (Cake will shrink if removed from pan while warm.) Insert spatula between cake and side of pan until tip touches bottom. Press gently against side of pan, cutting away clinging cake. Pull spatula out; repeat all around edge and tube. Invert cake on wire rack and lift off pan.

11. Serve in wedges as is, or topped with strawberries. Or split into 2 layers and fill with whipped cream and sliced peaches or strawberries.

ANGEL-FOOD CAKE

1¼ cups egg whites (10 to 12 eggs)	¼ teaspoon salt
1 cup plus 2 tablespoons sifted cake flour	1¼ teaspoons cream of tartar
1½ cups sifted granulated sugar	1 teaspoon vanilla extract
	¼ teaspoon almond extract

1. Set out egg whites to come to room temperature—about 1 hour.

2. Start heating oven to 375°F.

3. Sift flour with ½ cup sugar 4 times.

4. In large bowl combine egg whites, salt, cream of tartar, and extracts. With mixer at high speed (or with hand beater or flat wire whip), beat egg whites until stiff enough to hold soft, moist peaks.

5. With mixer at same speed, beat in 1 cup sugar, sprinkling ¼ cup at a time over egg whites. Beat until just blended. (To beat by hand, beat 25 strokes or turns, after each addition.) Stop mixer.

6. Sift in flour mixture in fourths, folding in each addition with 15 complete fold-over strokes of spoon, rubber spatula, or wire whip, turning bowl often. After all flour has been folded in, give batter 10 to 20 extra strokes. Gently push batter into ungreased 10-inch tube pan. With spatula, cut through batter without lifting spatula out of batter.

7. Bake 30 to 35 minutes, or until cake tester, inserted in center, comes out clean.

8. Cool and remove from pan as in step 10 of Sponge-cake recipe, above. Frost as desired, or serve in wedges, sprinkled with confectioners' sugar.

FRUIT CAKELETS

4 cups sifted regular all-purpose flour	½ pound whole candied cherries
3 teaspoons double-acting baking powder	1 15-ounce package light raisins
1 teaspoon salt	1½ cups canned slivered toasted almonds
½ teaspoon ground nutmeg	1 7-ounce package fine grated coconut
½ pound diced preserved citron	1½ cups butter or margarine
½ pound diced preserved orange peel	1½ cups granulated sugar
½ pound diced preserved pineapple	1 cup pineapple juice
	10 egg whites, unbeaten

1. Buy about 100 pink, green, gold, silver, and blue foil nut cups. Place them either in cupcake-pan cups or on cookie sheets.

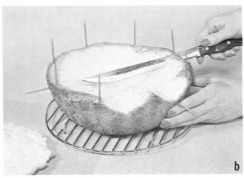

Petal Cake

2.   Sift flour with baking powder, salt, and nutmeg.
3.   In large 4½-quart bowl or pan, mix citron, orange peel, pineapple, cherries, raisins, and almonds with coconut; add flour mixture; stir to coat fruits well. as in *photo a, page 42.*
4.   In another 4½-quart bowl work butter with mixer or spoon until creamy; gradually beat in sugar until light and fluffy. Stir in fruit mixture alternately with pineapple juice, beginning and ending with fruit mixture.
5.   Start heating oven to 325°F.
6.   Beat egg whites until stiff; carefully fold into batter until no egg-white flecks remain as in *photo b, page 42.* Put rounded measuring tablespoonful of batter into each foil cup as in *photo c, page 42,* pushing and leveling with small spatula.
7.   Bake 40 minutes, or until done.
8.   Cool on wire rack; repeat bakings until all batter is used. When cakelets are cool, wrap, then refrigerate until needed. Makes about 100.

PETAL CAKE

*1 package angel-food- or
   chiffon-cake mix*
3 pints favorite ice creams

*1 package fluffy-white-
   frosting mix*
Green food color
Fruits and walnut halves

1.   Start heating oven to 350°F.
2.   In 3-quart ovenproof bowl, make up cake mix as label directs.

3.   Bake cake in same bowl 45 minutes, or until done.
4.   To cool cake, invert bowl with edges resting on 2 inverted cake pans. With long spatula, carefully loosen cake on all sides; remove from bowl and cool on wire rack.
5.   Meanwhile, using number 16 scoop, make 12 ice-cream balls from 3 or more favorite flavors. Store on cookie sheet in freezer until needed.
6.   Now, with sharp knife at an angle and starting 1 inch in from top edge of cake, cut down and around cake, then remove shallow cone-shaped piece as in *photo a.* Brush off all loose crumbs.
7.   Around top edge of cake place 8 toothpicks, 3½ inches apart and at right angle to edge. Between every 2 picks and 1 inch below, center a pick. Starting with one of picks at top edge, make diagonal cut down to lower pick, then a cut from next top pick to same lower pick; lift out wedge as in *photo b.* Repeat all the way around to make 8 petals.
8.   Make up frosting mix as label directs; tint a delicate green. Invert cake on inverted bowl; lightly frost to set crumbs. With small spatula and rest of frosting make three strokes on each petal. Let frosting set.
Just before serving:
Set cake, right side up, on cake stand. Fill with ice-cream balls; garnish with favorite fruits and walnuts as pictured. To serve, lift ice-cream balls from one petal to dessert plate, then cut out petal to set beside them. Makes 8 servings.

Pies

The success of many pies depends upon the pastry. Only top-notch ingredients and streamlined techniques make it possible to turn out masterpieces "as easy as pie." Start with Susan's Perfect Pie Shell, or use one of the packaged piecrust mixes.

PERFECT PIE SHELL

1½ cups sifted regular all-purpose | *½ cup vegetable shortening*
flour | *¼ cup cold water*
½ teaspoon salt

Several hours ahead:

1. In bowl mix flour with salt. With pastry blender, or 2 knives, cut shortening into flour until size of peas as in *photo a*.
2. Combine about ¼ cup flour mixture with water. Add it to rest of flour mixture as in *photo b*. With fork or fingers, mix until dough holds together. Shape dough into flat round.
3. On lightly floured pastry cloth, with stockinet-covered rolling pin, roll dough lightly from center out to edge in all directions, forming a circle about 1½ inches wider all around than an inverted 8- or 9-inch pie plate. In rolling, lift rolling pin near edge of circle to keep edge from splitting or getting too thin. If edge splits, pinch cracks together. If pastry sticks, loosen gently with spatula, lift it and lightly flour surface of cloth.
4. Fold pastry circle in half, then lift onto 8- or 9-inch pie plate as in *photo c*, with fold at center. Gently unfold and fit into plate, being careful not to stretch it.
5. Trim pastry to about 1 inch beyond edge of pie plate. Fold overhang under pastry so it extends slightly beyond plate edge. Firmly place right index finger on inside of pastry rim; with left thumb and index finger pinch pastry at that point, as in *photo d*. Repeat all around rim, making sure points hook over plate edge.
6. With 4-tined fork, prick pastry well on bottom and side as in *photo e*. Refrigerate 30 minutes
7. Start heating oven to 450°F.
8. Bake pastry 12 to 15 minutes, or until it is golden. After 5 minutes, peek to see if bubbles appear; prick with fork.
9. Cool pie shell before filling. If recipe calls for unbaked pie shell, omit pricking and baking as above. Fill and bake as specified in recipe. Makes 1 8- or 9-inch pie shell.

LEMON PARFAIT PIE

1 baked 8-inch pie shell (Perfect | *1¼ cups hot water*
Pie Shell, above, or piecrust mix) | *1 teaspoon grated lemon peel*
1 3-ounce package lemon-flavor | *3 tablespoons lemon juice*
gelatin | *1 pint vanilla ice cream*

1. Make and bake pie shell as recipe (or package label) directs.
2. In 2-quart saucepan dissolve gelatin in hot water; add lemon peel and juice.
3. Add ice cream by spoonfuls, stirring until melted. Refrigerate until thickened but not set—25 to 30 minutes.
4. Turn into pie shell. Refrigerate until firm—25 to 35 minutes.

LIME-PINEAPPLE PIE: Make and bake 9-inch pie shell. Substitute

lime-flavor gelatin for lemon. Drain juice from 1 1-pound 4-ounce can crushed pineapple. Add enough water to juice to measure 1¼ cups. Heat and use to dissolve gelatin. Omit lemon peel and juice. At end of step 3, fold in 1 cup crushed pineapple (reserve rest for garnish). Refrigerate as above.

SLIPPED CUSTARD PIE

1 baked 9-inch pie shell (Perfect Pie Shell, page 44, or piecrust mix)	½ teaspoon salt
	1 teaspoon vanilla extract
	2 cups milk
4 eggs, slightly beaten	½ teaspoon nutmeg
½ cup granulated sugar	

Early on day:
1. Make and bake pie shell as recipe (or package label) directs; cool.
2. Start heating oven to 350°F.
3. Combine eggs, sugar, salt, vanilla, milk, and nutmeg; beat well.
4. Grease well a second 9-inch pie plate; set in shallow baking pan. Pour egg mixture into pie plate; set in oven. Pour enough hot water into baking pan to come halfway up side of pie plate.
5. Bake 35 minutes, or until silver knife, inserted in center, comes out clean.
6. *Cool well on wire rack at room temperature.*
7. Now, tilt custard a bit. With small spatula, gently pull custard away from sides of pie plate all the way around. Then, holding pie plate level with both hands, shake gently. Tilt plate with far edge just above and close to far edge of baked pie shell; shake gently; as custard slips out, gently pull plate back until all custard rests in pie shell.
8. Let pie settle a few minutes; then serve at once, or refrigerate until served.

COCONUT CUSTARD PIE: Just before or after baking, sprinkle custard with ½ cup flaked coconut.

FUDGE-NUT PIE

1 package piecrust mix	¼ teaspoon salt
2 squares unsweetened chocolate	½ cup milk
	¼ cup corn or maple-flavored syrup
½ cup light-brown sugar, packed	
¼ cup butter or margarine	1 cup finely chopped walnuts
¾ cup granulated sugar	
3 eggs, unbeaten	1 teaspoon vanilla extract
	¼ cup broken walnuts

1. Make up pastry as package label directs. Roll half of pastry into circle with diameter slightly larger than top of 9-inch pie plate; invert pie plate on pastry and with point of sharp knife trace around edge of plate. Pull off excess pastry; lift off plate. Fit circle of pastry into bottom and part way up sides of pie plate.

2. Roll out other half of pastry. With floured 2-inch cutter, cut into 20 rounds. Place a round on inside of pie plate so it overlaps bottom pastry and comes up a bit above rim of pie plate. Moisten one edge of this round with water; overlap it slightly with another pastry round, pressing it into place. Repeat all around pie plate, forming petals. Refrigerate.
3. Start heating oven to 350°F.
4. In double boiler, over hot, *not boiling*, water, melt chocolate. Remove double-boiler top from water; into chocolate stir brown sugar and butter. With mixer at high speed, or with spoon, beat until blended; add granulated sugar and beat again.
5. To chocolate mixture, add eggs, one at a time, beating well after each addition. Add salt, then combined milk and syrup; beat until foamy.
6. Replace double-boiler top over hot, *not boiling*, water; cook pie filling 5 minutes, stirring constantly. Remove from water; stir in chopped walnuts and vanilla. Pour into chilled, unbaked pie shell.
7. Bake 55 minutes. Then open oven, pull oven rack part way out, and sprinkle broken walnuts over pie. Bake 5 minutes longer.
8. Serve warm, topped with ice cream.
Note: Pie may be made day before, then refrigerated; to serve, heat at 350°F. about 15 minutes. Or make, bake, then freeze wrapped pie a week or so ahead; to serve, heat unwrapped frozen pie at 350°F. about 20 minutes.

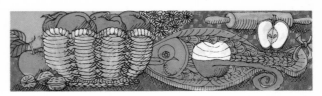

FRESH APPLE PIE

1 package piecrust mix	1 to 2 teaspoons lemon juice
⅔ to ¾ cup granulated sugar (or half granulated, half brown)	¼ teaspoon nutmeg
	½ teaspoon cinnamon
1 to 2 tablespoons flour (if fruit is juicy)	6 to 7 cups thinly sliced, cored, pared cooking apples (2 pounds)
⅛ teaspoon salt	
½ teaspoon grated lemon peel	1 tablespoon butter or margarine

1. Make up pastry as package label directs. Roll out half of pastry into circle about 1 inch larger than inverted 9-inch pie plate; use to line pie plate to form bottom crust; refrigerate.
2. Start heating oven to 425°F.
3. Combine sugar with flour, salt, lemon peel and juice, nutmeg, and cinnamon (amount of sugar depends on tartness of apples).

4. Place half of apples in pastry-lined pie plate, with sharp edges facing inward; sprinkle with half of sugar mixture. Top with rest of apples, heaping them in center; sprinkle with rest of sugar mixture. Dot with butter.

5. With kitchen scissors or knife, trim bottom pastry even with rim of pie plate. Moisten edge of pastry with water.

6. Roll out rest of pastry into 12-inch circle; fold in half. Make several slits near edge of fold. Lay pastry over apples, with fold at center; unfold. Fold edge of upper crust under edge of lower crust; press together. With floured 4-tined fork, press pastry to plate rim at ½-inch intervals.

7. Bake 40 to 50 minutes, or until filling is tender and crust nicely browned. Especially nice warm.

CHRISTMAS PIE

1½ cups finely-ground Brazil nuts	1¾ cups milk, scalded
3 tablespoons granulated sugar	½ cup thinly sliced glacéed cherries
1 envelope unflavored gelatin	2 tablespoons light rum
½ cup granulated sugar	3 egg whites, unbeaten
⅛ teaspoon salt	¼ cup shelled Brazil nuts
3 egg yolks, unbeaten	Boiling water
	¾ to 1 cup heavy cream

Day before, or early on day:
1. Start heating oven to 400°F.
2. Mix ground Brazil nuts with 3 tablespoons sugar. With back of spoon, press nut mixture to bottom and sides of 8-inch pie plate; *do not spread on rim.*
3. Bake 6 to 8 minutes, or until light brown; cool.
4. Make custard filling: In double boiler combine gelatin, ¼ cup sugar, and salt. Stir in egg yolks *well;* then *slowly* stir in scalded milk. Cook, over simmering water, stirring constantly, until mixture coats metal spoon. Remove from heat.
5. Cool custard filling; refrigerate until some of it mounds when dropped from spoon. (Or chill in bowl of ice water, stirring constantly.) With hand beater, beat until smooth; add cherries and rum.
6. Beat egg whites until soft peaks form when beater is slowly raised. Gradually add ¼ cup sugar, beating until stiff. Fold into custard mixture.
7. Pour all but 1 cup filling into cooled nut crust; refrigerate pie and reserved filling. When some of reserved filling mounds when dropped from spoon, heap on center of pie; refrigerate until serving time. (Allow about 4 hours to chill it firm enough to serve.)
8. Soak Brazil nuts in boiling water 30 minutes. With sharp paring knife, shave nuts to sprinkle over pie.
At serving time:
Whip cream, sweetened, if desired; spoon around top outer edge of pie. Garnish with shaved Brazil nuts.

HEAVENLY PIE

1½ cups granulated sugar	1 tablespoon grated lemon peel
¼ teaspoon cream of tartar	3 tablespoons lemon juice
4 egg whites, unbeaten	⅛ teaspoon salt
3 tablespoons canned flaked coconut (optional)	2 cups heavy cream (1 pint)
4 egg yolks, unbeaten	Strawberries

Make pie day before:
1. Start heating oven to 275°F.
2. Sift 1 cup sugar with cream of tartar.
3. With mixer at medium speed, or with hand beater, beat egg whites until stiff, but not dry. Slowly add sugar mixture, beating until very stiff and glossy.
4. Spread this meringue over bottom and up sides, just to rim, of well-greased 9-inch pie plate, making bottom ¼ inch thick, sides 1 inch thick. Sprinkle with 2 tablespoons coconut.
5. Bake 1 hour; meringue shell should be light brown and crisp; cool. (Toast remaining coconut while meringue bakes.)
6. Meanwhile, in top of double boiler beat egg yolks slightly; stir in ½ cup sugar, lemon peel and juice, and salt. Cook, over boiling water, stirring, until thickened—about 8 to 10 minutes; cool.
7. Whip 1 cup cream; fold into cooled lemon mixture. Pour into center of cooled meringue shell, making sure all pockets are filled. Smooth top. Refrigerate at least 12 hours, preferably 24 hours.
At serving time:
Top pie with 1 cup heavy cream, whipped; then sprinkle with toasted coconut and garnish with strawberries.

FROZEN CHOCOLATE VELVET PIE

8-inch pie:
2 egg whites, unbeaten
⅛ teaspoon salt
¼ cup granulated sugar
2 cups finely chopped walnuts
¼ cup white corn syrup
1 tablespoon water
1 tablespoon vanilla extract
1 cup semisweet-chocolate pieces
⅔ cup chilled canned sweetened
   condensed milk
1½ cups heavy cream

10-inch pie:
3 egg whites, unbeaten
¼ teaspoon salt
6 tablespoons granulated sugar
3 cups finely chopped walnuts
6 tablespoons white corn syrup
4 teaspoons water
5 teaspoons vanilla extract
1½ cups semisweet-chocolate
   pieces
1 cup chilled canned sweetened
   condensed milk
2 cups heavy cream

Make and freeze up to 1 month ahead:

1. Start heating oven to 400°F.
2. Beat egg whites with salt until soft peaks form when beater is slowly raised. Gradually beat in sugar; beat until stiff peaks form. Add nuts. Spread mixture over bottom and up sides of greased 8- or 10-inch pie plate, making rim ¾-inch high as in *photo a*.
3. Bake pie shell 12 minutes; cool.
4. Meanwhile, bring corn syrup and water just to boil, stirring. Remove from heat; stir in vanilla, then chocolate until it is melted; cool. Reserve 2 tablespoons this chocolate mixture; pour rest into large bowl with condensed milk and cream. With mixer at low speed, blend mixture well; at medium speed, beat until soft peaks form when beater is slowly raised as in *photo b*.
5. Pour filling into cooled pie shell. Place, unwrapped, in freezer until firm. When pie is firm, pipe on reserved chocolate, using decorating bag and plain writing tube, as in *photo c*. Freezer-wrap and freeze up to 1 month.

Frozen Chocolate Velvet Pie

About 25 minutes before serving:
Remove pie from freezer to wire rack to soften slightly. Cut into small wedges (10 to 12 from 8-inch pie; 16 from 10-inch pie), dipping knife in warm water occasionally so wedges cut smoothly. Serve with an assortment of fruits.

QUICK LEMON PRETZEL PIE

1 3-ounce package lemon-flavor gelatin
1½ cups boiling water
1 pint vanilla ice cream
½ teaspoon ground ginger
2 teaspoons grated lemon peel
¼ cup soft butter or margarine
3 tablespoons granulated sugar
¾ cup medium-fine pretzel crumbs (from packaged thin pretzels, miniature pretzels, or thin pretzel sticks)

Early on day, or several hours ahead:
1.   Place gelatin in medium bowl; pour in boiling water, stirring until gelatin is dissolved. Stir in ice cream until all is blended. Add ginger and lemon peel.
2.   Partially fill large bowl with ice cubes and water; set bowl of gelatin mixture into it as in *photo a*, to hasten setting. If kitchen is very warm, place both bowls in refrigerator. As gelatin mixture begins to set around edges, stir occasionally.
3.   Meanwhile, in ungreased 8-inch pie plate, combine butter, sugar, and pretzel crumbs until well blended. With back of spoon, press mixture against bottom and sides of pie plate as in *photo b*. Refrigerate.
4.   When gelatin mixture has just set, beat with mixer or hand beater until smooth. Replace in bowl of ice water for a few minutes until it becomes stiff enough to mound. Spoon mixture into chilled crust as in *photo c*. Refrigerate pie several hours.
5.   Garnish pie with whole pretzel as in *photo d*, or several broken pretzel sticks. Cut into 6 to 8 wedges.

STRAWBERRY CHEESE PIE

1 cup sifted regular all-purpose flour
¼ cup granulated sugar
1 teaspoon grated lemon peel
½ cup butter or margarine, cut into pieces
1 egg yolk, unbeaten
¼ teaspoon vanilla extract
2½ 8-ounce packages soft cream cheese (20 ounces)
1 cup granulated sugar
1½ tablespoons flour
⅛ teaspoon salt
¼ teaspoon grated lemon peel
¼ teaspoon grated orange peel
3 eggs, unbeaten
1 egg white, unbeaten
2 tablespoons heavy cream or evaporated milk
¼ teaspoon vanilla extract
1 quart strawberries, washed, hulled
¾ cup currant jelly, melted

Day before, or early on day:
1.   In bowl, mix together 1 cup flour, ¼ cup sugar, and 1 teaspoon lemon peel. Make well in center and drop in pieces of butter. Add egg yolk and ¼ teaspoon vanilla. With fork, work butter into flour until dough is soft and pliable. Press dough into ball.
2.   With back of spoon, press two thirds of dough evenly over bottom of 10-inch pie plate; press rest around sides—not up on rim. Refrigerate several hours or overnight.
At baking time:
1.   Start heating oven to 400°F.

. Prick chilled pie shell with fork on bottom and
[si]des.

. Bake 7 minutes; cool. Increase oven heat to 450°F.

. With mixer at medium speed, or with spoon, beat
[c]heese until fluffy. Slowly add combined 1 cup sugar,
½ tablespoons flour, salt, lemon and orange peels, beat-
[in]g until fluffy. Beat in eggs and egg white, one at a
[ti]me. Beat in cream and vanilla. Pour most of filling
[in]to cooled crust. To avoid spilling, set filled pie on oven
[ra]ck; add rest of filling.

. Bake 7 minutes, or until crust is golden. Reduce
[o]ven heat to 200°F. and bake 15 minutes longer (it will
[b]e puffy and set).

. Cool pie on wire rack away from draft. (Don't
[w]orry, it will shrink, and may crack a little as it cools.)

. Arrange well-drained strawberries over entire sur-
[f]ace of cooled pie. Carefully spoon cooled, melted jelly
[o]ver berries. Refrigerate until serving time.

[S]TRAWBERRY TARTS

quart fresh strawberries,   ¼ teaspoon cinnamon
tablespoon lemon juice   Light cream
[½] cup granulated sugar   1 8-ounce package soft
tablespoon cornstarch   cream cheese*
package piecrust mix   3 tablespoons milk
[?] tablespoons granulated   1 teaspoon grated lemon
   sugar   peel

. In saucepan crush 1 cup strawberries with wooden
[s]poon. Add lemon juice, ½ cup sugar, and cornstarch.
[C]ook over low heat, stirring, until thickened and clear.
[S]et aside to cool.

[2]. Make up piecrust mix as label directs, adding 2 ta-
[b]lespoons sugar and cinnamon, and substituting cream
[f]or water called for.

[3]. Start heating oven to 450°F.

[4]. Roll out pastry ⅛ inch thick; cut out 6 5-inch
[r]ounds. Over back of 3-inch muffin-pan cup fit a pastry
[r]ound, making 6 pleats in it; repeat on alternate muffin
[c]ups. With 4-tined fork, prick shells on bottom.

[5]. Bake 5 minutes, or until golden; cool on wire rack.

[6]. Carefully fold remaining whole berries into cooled
[b]erry mixture until all are glazed.

[7]. Mix cream cheese with milk and lemon peel; spoon
[in]to cooled shells. With teaspoons, carefully lift each
[b]erry out of sauce and heap on cheese filling, dividing
[t]hem equally among 6 tarts. Drizzle any remaining
[s]yrup over them. Makes 6 tarts.

[*]One package vanilla-pudding-and-pie-filling mix, made
[a]s label directs, may replace cheese filling.

[N]ote: Tarts may be made any time of year by substitut-
[i]ng well-drained, thawed frozen whole strawberries;
[d]rained canned or thawed frozen peaches or blue-
[b]erries; or fresh or frozen raspberries for the fresh
[s]trawberries.

Desserts

CUSTARD BREAD PUDDING

1 quart milk
2 cups 2-day-old bread
   crumbs or ½-inch
   squares
2 eggs, unbeaten
¼ cup granulated sugar
½ teaspoon salt
¼ teaspoon nutmeg
1 tablespoon vanilla extract,
   or 1 teaspoon almond
   extract
2 to 4 tablespoons melted
   butter or margarine

1. Start heating oven to 350°F.

2. In double boiler, heat milk until tiny bubbles appear around edges. Remove from heat; stir in bread
crumbs; set aside.

3. Break eggs into greased 1½-quart casserole; beat
slightly with fork. Stir in sugar, salt, then milk mixture,
nutmeg, vanilla, and butter.

4. Set casserole in baking pan; fill pan with enough
warm water to within 1 inch of top of casserole.

5. Bake, uncovered, 1 hour and 15 minutes, or until
silver knife, inserted in center, comes out clean.

6. Serve warm or cold, with pour cream; whipped
cream; lemon sauce; hard sauce; sweetened crushed
strawberries, flavored with almond extract; or top with
bits of jelly. Makes 6 to 8 servings.

FOR 2 OR 3: Halve each ingredient; use 1-quart casserole or 4 custard cups. Bake as directed 45 to 50 minutes,
or until it tests done.

CAKE CRUMB: Substitute stale cake crumbs for bread
crumbs. Bake as directed.

CHOCOLATE NUT: In heated milk, melt 2 squares unsweetened chocolate; with hand beater, beat until
blended; add ½ cup chopped walnuts.

COCONUT: Before baking pudding, sprinkle top with ½
cup flaked coconut.

RAISIN OR DATE: With milk mixture, add ½ cup light
or dark raisins, or snipped, pitted dates.

QUEEN OF PUDDINGS: Use 2 eggs and 2 egg yolks.
Bake in 6 to 8 greased 5-ounce custard cups, in pan of
warm water, 45 to 50 minutes, or until a silver knife,
inserted in center, comes out clean. Remove from oven.
Beat 2 leftover egg whites until soft peaks form when
beater is slowly raised; slowly add ¼ cup granulated
sugar, beating until stiff. Heap on top of puddings,
leaving depression in center top of each. Bake, in pan
of warm water, at 350°F. 12 to 15 minutes, or until
golden. Serve warm or cold, with dab of currant jelly
in center of each. Or spread jelly on puddings before
topping with meringue.

RICE CUSTARD PUDDING

½ cup uncooked regular
  rice
3 eggs, unbeaten
⅓ cup granulated sugar
2 teaspoons vanilla extract
½ cup light or dark raisins

1½ teaspoons grated lemon
  peel
3½ cups milk
1 teaspoon nutmeg
2 tablespoons butter or
  margarine

1. Star heating oven to 300°F.
2. Cook rice until tender, as package label directs.
3. Into 2-quart casserole, break eggs; beat slightly with fork. Stir in sugar, vanilla, raisins, and lemon peel.
4. Stir milk into rice; stir into egg mixture. Sprinkle with nutmeg; then dot with butter. Set casserole in baking pan; fill pan with hot water up to within 1 inch of top of casserole.
5. Bake, uncovered, 1 hour and 25 minutes, stirring once after 30 minutes. (To avoid breaking top, insert spoon at edge of casserole; draw gently back and forth along bottom of casserole.) Near end of baking time, insert silver knife in center. If it comes out clean, pudding is done.
6. Remove casserole from baking pan; cool. Serve, slightly warm or cold, with pour cream; whipped cream; maple or maple-blended syrup; hot fudge sauce; or butterscotch sauce. Makes 6 to 8 servings.
FOR 2 OR 3: Use 3 tablespoons rice, 2 small eggs, 3 tablespoons sugar; halve rest of ingredients. Use a 1-quart casserole. Bake 55 minutes.

CARAMEL-TOPPED CUSTARD

½ cup granulated sugar
4 eggs, unbeaten
¼ teaspoon salt
1½ cups milk

½ cup light cream
1 teaspoon vanilla extract
Chopped walnuts or flaked
  coconut

About 4 hours before serving:
1. In small skillet, over medium heat, melt ¼ cup sugar, stirring until it forms a caramel-like syrup. Immediately spoon into 6 buttered 5-ounce custard cups as in *photo a.*
2. Start heating oven to 300°F.

3. Into bowl, break eggs. With mixer at medium speed, beat eggs until fluffy. Add ¼ cup sugar and salt, beating until thick and lemon-colored. Stir in milk, cream, and vanilla well; let any foam settle.
4. Set custard cups in open baking pan; fill pan with hot water to within ¾ inch of top. Pour custard through fine strainer, into each cup as in *photo b,* filling to within ½ inch of top.
5. Bake 1 hour and 10 minutes, or until silver knife, inserted in center, comes out clean as in *photo c.*
6. Remove custards from oven to wire rack; cool, then refrigerate.
7. To serve, run spatula around inside of each custard cup; place dessert plate, upside down, on top of each cup; then invert to unmold. Garnish each with walnuts. Makes 6 servings.
MAPLE-TOPPED CUSTARD: Place 1 tablespoon maple, maple-flavored, or buttered syrup in each custard cup before pouring in custard.
MARSHMALLOW-TOPPED CUSTARD: Place 1 large marshmallow in each custard cup before pouring in custard.

SNOW PUDDING

2 teaspoons unflavored
  gelatin
¼ cup cold water
¾ cup granulated sugar
Pinch salt
1 cup hot water

1 teaspoon grated lemon
  or lime peel
¼ cup lemon or lime juice
3 egg whites, unbeaten
Custard Sauce, page 51

1. In large bowl, sprinkle gelatin over cold water to soften. Add ½ cup sugar, salt, and hot water; stir until gelatin is dissolved. Add lemon peel and juice; stir until blended. Refrigerate, stirring often, until consistency of unbeaten egg white.
2. With mixer at medium speed, or hand beater, beat egg whites until they form moist peaks when beater is slowly raised. Gradually add ¼ cup sugar, beating until stiff. Add to gelatin mixture, beating until thoroughly combined. Turn into 1-quart mold; refrigerate until set.
3. Unmold onto serving dish. Or refrigerate in bowl

until set, then pile in sherbet dishes. Serve with Custard Sauce. Makes 4 or 5 servings.

CUSTARD SAUCE: In double boiler heat 1 cup milk until tiny bubbles appear around edges. In medium bowl, beat 3 egg yolks slightly with fork; stir in 1½ to 2 tablespoons granulated sugar and ⅛ teaspoon salt. Add hot milk slowly, stirring constantly. Return mixture to double boiler; cook over hot, *not boiling*, water, stirring constantly until thick enough to coat spoon. Pour *at once* into cool bowl; cool; add ½ teaspoon vanilla. Cover; refrigerate until chilled.

EGGS À LA NEIGE

4 cups milk
6 egg whites, unbeaten
1¼ cups granulated sugar
Salt
1½ cups heavy cream
¾ teaspoon vanilla extract
6 egg yolks, unbeaten
1½ tablespoons flour
2 pints fresh strawberries
1 square unsweetened chocolate

Day before, or early on day:

1. In large skillet heat milk until scalded.

2. Meanwhile, beat egg whites until frothy; gradually add ¾ cup sugar and ¼ teaspoon salt, beating until stiff.

3. Onto hot milk in skillet, drop 3 large mounds of meringue, 1 inch apart, as in *photo a;* cook 5 minutes, turning once with slotted spoon. Drain on paper towel. Repeat until all meringue is used; refrigerate meringues.

4. In double boiler, scald cream with vanilla and 1½ cups of milk used for meringues.

5. Meanwhile, beat egg yolks until light; beat in ½ cup sugar, pinch salt, flour, and a little of hot milk-cream mixture. Stir this into rest of hot milk-cream mixture. Cook over hot, *not boiling*, water, stirring, until sauce coats metal spoon.

6. Cool sauce and meringues in refrigerator until 20 minutes before serving. Then, hull, wash, and slice strawberries into deep serving dish. On them heap meringues, then pour on sauce. With vegetable parer, shave chocolate over all as in *photo b*. Makes 8 servings.

To vary: Substitute sliced peaches or bananas or any fruit of your choice for strawberries. Or serve Eggs à la Neige in individual nappy dishes; omit fruit.

Eggs à la Neige

CROWNING-GLORY ORANGE SOUFFLÉ

Soufflé:
Salad oil or soft butter
2 envelopes unflavored gelatin
½ cup cold water
8 eggs, at room temperature
1¼ cups granulated sugar
½ cup finely grated orange peel
3 tablespoons finely-grated lemon
   peel
1 teaspoon salt

¾ cup orange juice
¼ cup lemon juice
2 cups heavy cream

Garnish:
3 medium oranges, sectioned
¼ cup currant jelly
1 envelope unflavored gelatin
¼ cup cold water
Red food color

About 5 hours before serving:
1.   With cellophane tape, fasten 30-by-6-inch band of foil around top outside of 1½-quart soufflé dish as in *photo a,* so foil stands about 4 inches above rim; tape inside and outside seams of foil, then brush inside of foil with salad oil.
2.   In small bowl, sprinkle gelatin onto ½ cup water. Set over hot water, stirring until gelatin is dissolved.
3.   Separate eggs, placing yolks in double-boiler top and whites in large bowl. To yolks, add ½ cup sugar, orange and lemon peels, salt, and orange and lemon juices. With hand beater, beat until fluffy. Cook, over simmering water, stirring constantly, until thickened as in *photo b.* Stir in dissolved gelatin. Remove from heat; cool, over ice, stirring constantly, until it *just begins to mound.*
4.   Beat egg whites until frothy; gradually add ¾ cup sugar, beating until soft peaks form when beater is slowly raised. Now whip cream; pile it on egg whites. Then fold in custard as in *photo c,* until no large areas of white remain. Spoon carefully into soufflé dish; refrigerate 3 hours, or until set.
5.   Meanwhile, fix garnish: Dry orange sections on paper towels. In saucepan, melt jelly. Sprinkle gelatin over cold water to soften; stir over hot water until gelatin is dissolved. Add 1 tablespoon gelatin to jelly; tint with few drops red food color. When jelly mixture cools, dip each orange section in it; drain orange sections on wire rack as in *photo d.*
6.   To serve, remove foil. Arrange orange sections on top of soufflé as pictured. Makes 10 to 12 servings.

CRÈME BRÛLÉE

3 cups heavy cream
6 egg yolks, unbeaten
6 tablespoons granulated sugar

1 teaspoon vanilla extract
½ cup light- or dark-brown sugar
Choice of fruit

Early on day:
1.   Place cream in bottom of double boiler; heat until tiny bubbles appear around edges.
2.   In top of double boiler, beat egg yolks with granulated sugar until blended. Slowly stir in scalded cream.
3.   Wash bottom of double boiler; fill with sufficient hot water; place top over hot water and cook egg mixture, over hot, *not boiling,* water, stirring constantly, until mixture is thick as heavy cream and coats back of spoon.
4.   Add vanilla; pour mixture into 1½-quart soufflé dish. Refrigerate until needed.

Crowning-Glory Orange Soufflé

Several hours before serving:
1. Preheat broiler 10 minutes, or as manufacturer directs.
2. Place brown sugar in fine strainer. While stirring with wooden spoon, sprinkle sugar over entire surface of brûlée.
3. Broil brûlée, about 3 inches from heat, a minute or so, or until sugar melts, making a shiny caramel-like top. Refrigerate.
To serve:
1. Place soufflé dish in center of large tray, with one or more fruits around it: sweetened fresh strawberries; fresh, thawed frozen, or canned pineapple chunks; raspberries; fresh or canned peach halves; canned or cooked pears; orange chunks; or tender pitted prunes.
2. Over each serving of fruit spoon some of brûlée. Makes 6 to 8 servings.

CHARLOTTE RUSSE SUPREME

2 cups milk
2 envelopes unflavored gelatin
¾ cup granulated sugar
¼ teaspoon salt
4 eggs, separated
1 tablespoon rum extract

2 cups heavy cream
Ladyfingers, split
2 dozen assorted cream mint
  patties
Chocolate sauce (from jar)

Night before, or early on day:
1. Scald milk. Meanwhile, in double boiler, mix gelatin, sugar, and salt; stir in egg yolks. Gradually add scalded milk and rum extract. Cook, over simmering water, stirring, until mixture coats metal spoon. Transfer custard to medium bowl. Set in large bowl of ice cubes, stirring occasionally, until mixture *just begins to mound* as in *photo a;* remove from ice.
2. Beat egg whites until stiff; fold in custard, then cream, whipped. Fill 2-quart mold to within 2 inches of top with custard; refrigerate 10 minutes. Next, line mold with ladyfingers as in *photo b,* pressing slightly into custard; pour in rest of custard. Refrigerate 3 hours, or overnight. With scissors, trim ladyfingers level with russe.
3. To unmold, loosen all around top with thin-bladed spatula; invert mold on serving plate. Wrap outside of mold with dishcloth, wrung out of hot water, until dessert loosens and mold can be lifted off as in *photo c.* Return dessert to refrigerator until serving time (not more than 1 hour later).
Just before serving:
Arrange row of mint patties around edge of serving plate. Drizzle chocolate sauce over top of russe as in *photo d.* Serve immediately, passing rest of sauce in pitcher. Makes 9 to 12 servings.

CHOCOLATE CINNAMON ICE CREAM

4 squares unsweetened chocolate
2 14-ounce cans sweetened
  condensed milk
1 quart light cream
2 cups water
2 tablespoons vanilla extract
¼ teaspoon salt

2 teaspoons cinnamon
About 15 pounds crushed ice
About 5 pounds ice-cream salt
1 4-ounce package German's sweet
  cooking chocolate, pounded into
  fine pieces (optional)

Early on day:
Read instructions for use of 4-quart electric ice-cream freezer.

Chocolate Cinnamon Ice Cream

About 3 or 4 hours before serving:
1. Melt unsweetened chocolate in double boiler; stir in condensed milk. Cook, over boiling water, stirring constantly, 5 minutes. Pour into large bowl; cool.
2. Meanwhile, pour boiling water over ice-cream can, cover, and dasher; let cool as instructed.
3. Into cooled chocolate mixture, with wire whip or large fork, blend cream, a little at a time; when smooth, blend in water, then vanilla, salt, and cinnamon.
4. Fit dasher into can; pour in ice-cream mixture. Place can in freezer bucket; fit lid and motor on top, then start motor. Fill freezer bucket with alternating layers of crushed ice and ice-cream salt as in *photo a*, using 8 cups ice for every 1 cup salt.
5. After ice cream has been freezing 15 minutes, pour in sweet chocolate, if desired.
6. When motor slows or stops—in about 10 to 15 minutes—spoon out salt and ice down to 2 inches below can lid, to wipe off lid and remove it. Remove dasher, then scrape ice cream from it with rubber spatula as in *photo b*. Pack ice cream down into can.
7. Replace lid; put cork in dasher hole and drain water from bucket. Repack bucket alternating ice and ice-cream salt, using 4 cups ice to every 1 cup salt. Cover with newspaper and let mellow for an hour or so. Makes 12 generous servings.
Note: Store any leftover ice cream, packed in tightly covered carton, in freezer.

MERINGUE SHELLS À LA MODE

3 egg whites, at room
   temperature
⅛ teaspoon cream of tartar
¾ cup granulated sugar
¾ teaspoon vanilla extract

About 1 quart favorite ice
   cream
Grated lemon peel
   (optional)
Melba Sauce, page 56

Several days ahead, or early on day:
1. Make Meringue Shells: In bowl, with mixer at high speed, beat egg whites until frothy. Sprinkle on cream of tartar, continuing to beat until egg whites are stiff but not dry. With measuring spoon, sprinkle in sugar, 2 tablespoons at a time, beating about 2 minutes after each addition. (This takes about 20 minutes in all.)
2. After sugar has been beaten in and meringue is thick, glossy, and straight peaks form when beater is slowly raised, beat in vanilla.
3. Start heating oven to 275°F.
4. With ice cream scoop number 12, or large spoon, drop 6 mounds of meringue onto buttered large cookie sheet. Repeat on second cookie sheet until all meringue is used. With small spatula, spread and shape each mound into a shell with depression in center, lifting meringue into small peaks.
5. Bake shells 45 minutes; reduce oven temperature to 250°F. and bake 15 minutes longer.
6. Cool on cookie sheets; wrap separately and set aside until serving.

  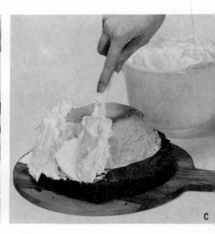

At serving time:
1. With number 12 ice cream scoop, scoop ice cream into as many balls as you have shells; sprinkle with lemon peel. Place on pan in freezer.
2. Make Melba Sauce. Place meringue shell on each dessert plate. Top with ice cream ball; spoon on Melba Sauce. Makes 7 or 8 servings.

MELBA SAUCE: In chafing dish or automatic skillet combine 1 10-ounce package frozen red raspberries, thawed and partially mashed, with ½ cup currant jelly; bring to boil, stirring. Add 1½ teaspoons cornstarch mixed with 1 tablespoon water; cook, stirring, until thickened.

BROWNIE BAKED ALASKA

2 pints coffee or strawberry ice cream
1 package fudge brownie mix
5 egg whites, unbeaten
10 tablespoons granulated sugar

A day ahead to 1 week before serving:
1. Line bowl, measuring about 7 inches across top, with wax paper, leaving overhang. Press ice cream into bottom of lined bowl; freeze.
2. Start heating oven as brownie-mix label directs.
3. Make up brownie mix as label directs for cake-like brownies. Turn into 8-by-1½-inch layer-cake pan that has been greased, then lined in bottom with wax paper.
4. Bake 5 minutes longer than label directs.
5. Cool in pan 15 minutes; then remove to wire rack.
6. When brownie is cool and ice cream is hard, with mixer at high speed, beat egg whites until frothy. Gradually beat in sugar, continuing to beat until meringue holds stiff peaks when beater is slowly raised.
7. Transfer brownie layer to board as in *photo a.* Loosen and lift ice cream from bowl; invert onto brownie layer and remove paper as in *photo b.*
8. Spread meringue completely over ice cream and brownie layer as in *photo c.* Freeze on board.

About 30 minutes before serving:
1. Start heating oven to 500°F.
2. Bake Alaska about 2 minutes, or until lightly browned.
3. Let stand about 10 minutes to soften slightly for serving. Cut into wedges with sturdy knife. Makes 12 servings.

STRAWBERRY SHORTCAKE

2 cups sifted regular all-purpose flour
3 teaspoons double-acting baking powder
¾ teaspoon salt
3 to 5 tablespoons granulated sugar
1 teaspoon grated lemon or orange peel (optional)
½ cup shortening
1 egg, beaten
About ⅓ cup milk
Butter or margarine
4 cups sweetened sliced or crushed strawberries
1 cup heavy cream

1. Start heating oven to 450°F.
2. Into bowl, sift flour with baking powder, salt, and sugar; add lemon or orange peel.
3. With pastry blender, or 2 knives, cut shortening into flour mixture until like corn meal. Add egg, then enough milk to make dough easy to handle.
4. Roll or pat dough into ½-inch-thick round, to fit greased 9-inch layer-cake pan. Or roll or pat dough ½-inch thick; cut into 3-inch rounds. Place, 1 inch apart, on cookie sheet.
5. Bake 12 to 15 minutes, or until done.
6. Split hot cake or cakes; butter well; fill with some of strawberries. Top with rest of berries, then with whipped cream. Makes 6 to 8 servings.

DROP BISCUIT SHORTCAKES: Increase milk in step 3 to about ½ cup. Drop dough into 6 to 8 3-inch mounds on greased cookie sheet. Bake 12 to 15 minutes, or until done.

To vary: Substitute one of these fruits for strawberries: sweetened crushed raspberries or blackberries; warm applesauce, topped with cinnamon-flavored whipped cream; sweetened, sliced fresh, or thawed frozen or canned peach slices; sliced bananas and drained canned fruit cocktail; half-and-half sweetened raspberries and strawberries or sliced bananas. Dessert topping may be used in place of whipped cream.

BANANA-SPLIT PANCAKES

3 or 4 bananas
1 cup packaged pancake mix
About ½ cup apricot preserves

½ cup chopped salted peanuts
1 pint vanilla ice cream

About 1 hour before serving:

1.   In small bowl, with fork, mash enough banana to measure ½ cup. Prepare pancake mix as package label directs, adding mashed banana with the egg.

2.   Heat electric griddle to temperature recommended for pancakes, or a regular griddle, over medium heat, until a drop of water "dances" when dropped on it.

3.   Lightly oil griddle or not, as manufacturer directs; pour batter onto it from ⅓-cup measure as in *photo a*. Let pancakes cook until bubbles form throughout and bottom is browned; then turn with broad spatula. Let cook on second side until they rise a little and are browned. (Turn only once!)

4.   Remove pancakes from griddle; stack on plate. Repeat step 3 until all of batter is used, making 8 pancakes in all.

5.   Beat apricot preserves with fork to soften. Peel 2 bananas; quarter them lengthwise. Brush quarters with some of apricot preserves, then roll in chopped nuts as in *photo b*, reserving any extra nuts. Lightly

Banana-Split Pancakes

Cranberry-Cheeseca

spread one side of each pancake with apricot preserves. Lay a banana quarter on each pancake and fold pancake around it. Arrange pancakes on a serving platter or two.

6.   Place a small scoop or spoonful of ice cream on each pancake; sprinkle ice cream with a few nuts as pictured on page 55. Serve as a hearty afternoon or evening snack. Makes 8 servings.

CRANBERRY-CHEESECAKE

1 cup packaged cornflake crumbs
2¼ cups granulated sugar
½ teaspoon cinnamon
3 tablespoons melted butter or margarine
4 8-ounce packages creamed cottage cheese
4 eggs, unbeaten
¼ cup regular all-purpose flour
½ cup heavy cream
1 tablespoon lemon juice
1 tablespoon vanilla extract
2 cups whole cranberries
1½ teaspoons unflavored gelatin

Day before:
1.   In bowl thoroughly combine cornflake crumbs with ¼ cup sugar, cinnamon, and butter. Use this mixture to cover bottom of 9-inch spring-form pan, packing it down firmly.
2.   Start heating oven to 350°F.
3.   With spoon, press cottage cheese through fine sieve into large bowl as in *photo a*. With mixer at high speed, beat in eggs, one at a time, beating well after each addition. Now, thoroughly beat in flour and 1 cup sugar as in *photo b*. Beat in cream, lemon juice, and vanilla, continuing to beat until very well blended. Pour into crumb-lined spring-form pan.

4.   Bake 50 minutes; turn off heat and leave cheesecake in oven 30 minutes longer.
5.   Remove from oven to wire rack to cool. (Cracks that may develop while cooling are characteristic.) Refrigerate overnight.

About 6 hours before serving:
1.   Prepare topping: In saucepan combine cranberries, ¾ cup water, and 1 cup sugar. Cook 5 minutes, or until skins pop, stirring occasionally.
2.   Meanwhile, soften gelatin in 2 tablespoons water. Stir into cranberry mixture until dissolved. Refrigerate just until mixture begins to thicken.
3.   Gently loosen cheesecake from sides of pan with spatula; carefully remove sides. Loosen cheesecake from bottom of pan; slowly slide it onto serving plate. Gently pour cranberry mixture onto cheesecake as in *photo c*, spreading over top of cake. Refrigerate until topping is set—about 3 hours.

Just before serving:
Cut cheesecake into wedges. Serve each wedge with a cracked walnut in the shell as pictured, if desired. Makes 16 servings.

NAPOLEONS

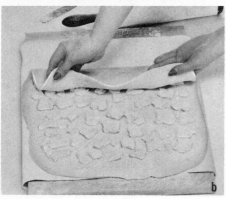

4½ cups sifted regular all-purpose
   flour
1 pound butter, chilled
Water
1 tablespoon vinegar

Custard Filling, page 61
1 cup sifted confectioners' sugar
¼ cup semisweet-chocolate pieces
1 teaspoon white corn syrup

Day before, or several days ahead:

1.   Into large bowl sift flour; add ½ pound butter in small pieces. With pastry blender, cut butter into flour as in *photo a,* until mixture is like corn meal.

2.   Mix 1 cup water with vinegar; pour over flour mixture. With fork, mix well; shape into ball. Wrap in foil or saran; refrigerate 30 minutes.

3.   On well-floured surface, with stockinet-covered rolling pin, roll dough into rectangle ¼-inch thick. Starting at narrow end of dough, dot two thirds of it with remaining ½ pound chilled butter. Fold unbuttered third over center third as in *photo b,* then fold last third on top, making three layers. Fold opposite ends so they completely overlap each other, making equal thirds and a block shape with straight sides. Wrap in foil; refrigerate 30 minutes.

4.   Reroll dough and repeat folding, wrapping, and refrigerating three more times.

Early on day:

1.   Remove dough from refrigerator; let rest 30 minutes.

2.   Now roll dough into rectangle 17 by 12 inches ¼-inch thick; let rest 30 minutes. Cut rolled out dough into 3 lengthwise strips, 4 inches wide as in *photo c, page 61.* Fold each in thirds; place on ungreased

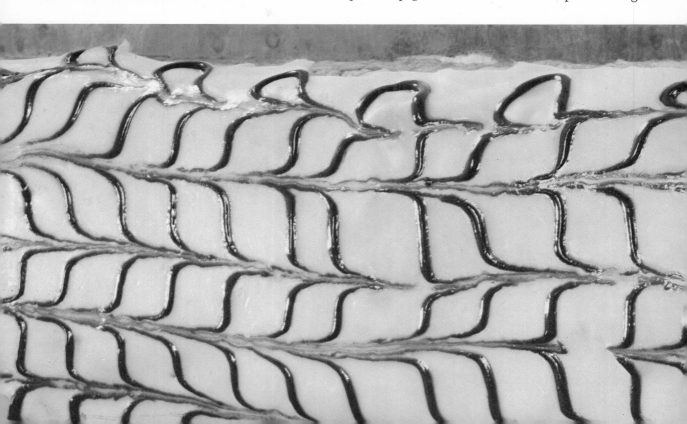

cookie sheets; unfold to original length. With fork, prick top of each strip. Refrigerate 30 minutes.

3. Start heating oven to 400°F.

4. Bake 50 to 55 minutes; *don't peek while baking.*

5. Cool on wire rack. Split each strip lengthwise. Freezer-wrap and freeze 3 strips for later use. Refrigerate others.

6. Make up Custard Filling; refrigerate.

A few hours before serving:

1. In small bowl, stir confectioners' sugar with 1 to 1½ tablespoons water until smooth. Over warm water, melt chocolate with corn syrup; stir in 1 teaspoon water; place in decorating bag with number 2 tube.

2. Lay pastry strips out in row. Frost one generously, using all of icing. With chocolate in decorating bag make zigzag lines crosswise, ½ inch apart, as in *photo d.* Then quickly, while frosting is still wet, draw tip of knife lengthwise through frosting and chocolate at ½-inch intervals to form zigzag design as pictured. Set decorated strip aside.

3. Cover second strip with half of filling; on it place third strip; cover with rest of filling. Top with decorated strip. Now, with very sharp knife, trim off any uneven edges. Refrigerate until serving. Makes 8.

CUSTARD FILLING: Scald 1½ cups milk. Beat 5 egg yolks well; beat in 6 tablespoons granulated sugar. Stir in ½ cup sifted regular all-purpose flour and scalded milk. In saucepan, heat, stirring, until custard is thickened; add 1½ tablespoons vanilla. Refrigerate until ready to assemble.

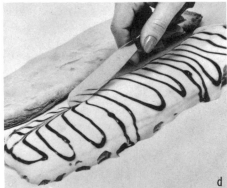

Napoleons

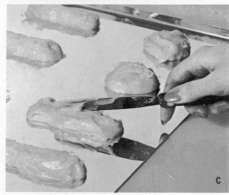

CHOCOLATE ÉCLAIRS

1 cup water
½ cup butter or margarine
½ teaspoon salt
1 cup sifted regular all-purpose
    flour
4 eggs, unbeaten

1 package vanilla- or chocolate-
    pudding-and-pie-filling mix
½ cup heavy cream
1 6-ounce package semisweet-
    chocolate pieces
2 tablespoons shortening

Early on day:

1.   Start heating oven to 400°F.

2.   In large saucepan combine water with butter and salt. Heat, over medium heat, until butter melts and water boils.

3.   Turn heat low; add flour, all at once, as in *photo a;* beat mixture vigorously with wooden spoon until it leaves sides of pan in a smooth, compact ball as in *photo b.*

4.   Immediately remove pan from heat; with wooden spoon, or portable mixer at medium speed, beat in eggs, one at a time, beating until smooth after each addition. When all eggs are blended, beat dough until very smooth and satiny.

5.   Drop dough, by heaping tablespoonfuls, about 2 inches apart, in rows 6 inches apart, onto large ungreased cookie sheets. With small spatula, spread each ball into 5-by-1-inch rectangle, with straight sides and smooth top as in *photo c.*

6.   Bake éclairs 35 to 40 minutes, or until brown.

7.   Loosen from cookie sheet with spatula and transfer to wire rack to cool.

8.   Meanwhile, prepare pudding mix as package label directs, using only 1½ cups milk. Place a piece of wax paper directly on surface of pudding; refrigerate.

9.   When pudding is cold, whip cream; beat pudding until smooth; fold in whipped cream. Split éclairs lengthwise, or slit and fold back tops; fill with pudding; replace tops. Set on wire rack.

10.   Now, in double boiler, over hot, *not boiling,* water, melt chocolate with shortening until smooth. Then, with wax paper under wire rack, spoon chocolate over éclairs as in *photo d,* spreading to cover. Refrigerate until serving time. Makes about 1 dozen.

CREAM PUFFS: Prepare dough as directed above. Drop mixture, by tablespoonfuls, 3 inches apart, onto greased cookie sheets, shaping each into a mound that points up in center. Bake 50 minutes; don't peek while baking. Cream puffs should be puffed high and golden. Remove with spatula to wire rack to cool. Split, fill, and top with chocolate as above. Or fill with Cream-Puff Filling, below; top with Thin Chocolate Glaze, page 63, then sprinkle with chopped nuts. Or fill with sugared strawberries; ice cream; sweetened whipped cream, flavored with almond, vanilla, or rum extract. Top with sifted confectioners' sugar, or hot butterscotch sauce, if desired. Makes 8 cream puffs.

FROZEN CREAM PUFFS: Make and bake cream puffs as directed. Fill with ice cream; freezer-wrap and freeze. (Will keep 3 or 4 weeks.) Slightly thaw in refrigerator before serving.

PETITE CREAM PUFFS: Drop dough, by rounded teaspoonfuls, onto lightly greased cookie sheet. Bake about 30 minutes. Cool, fill as desired and serve 2 per person.

CREAM-PUFF FILLING: In double-boiler top, mix ⅔ cup granulated sugar with ½ cup regular all-purpose flour and ¼ teaspoon salt. Stir in

2 eggs, slightly beaten, then 1½ cups scalded milk. Cook, over boiling water, 5 minutes, stirring constantly. Cook, stirring occasionally, 5 minutes longer. Refrigerate until cold. Add 2 teaspoons vanilla extract, fold in 1 cup heavy cream, whipped. Fills 8 cream puffs.

THIN CHOCOLATE GLAZE: Melt 2 tablespoons butter or margarine with 2 squares unsweetened chocolate and 2 tablespoons hot water over boiling water. Blend in 1 to 1½ cups sifted confectioners' sugar. With spoon, beat until smooth but not stiff.

CARAMEL APPLES

6 small apples   1 14-ounce bag caramels (49)
1 cup shelled walnuts

Day before, or several hours before serving:

1. Wash and dry apples; twist off any stems. Insert a wooden skewer part way into stem end of each. Set aside.
2. Chop walnuts fine; place on square of wax paper.
3. Unwrap caramels; place in double-boiler top with 3 tablespoons water. Melt caramels over boiling water as in *photo a,* stirring frequently until they form a smooth sauce.
4. Tilt double-boiler top with one hand; with other hand, hold an apple by the skewer and dip and twirl in caramel sauce to completely cover apple as in *photo b.* Replace double-boiler top and hold apple over sauce while twirling so sauce spreads smoothly over it.

5. When caramel sauce on apple just starts to dry, dip bottom half of apple in walnuts as in *photo c.* Place it, skewer side up, on wax-paper-covered cookie sheet or small tray. Repeat until all apples are coated; refrigerate until served.
6. Serve as a dessert or an after-school snack, or for a Halloween party. Makes 6 servings.

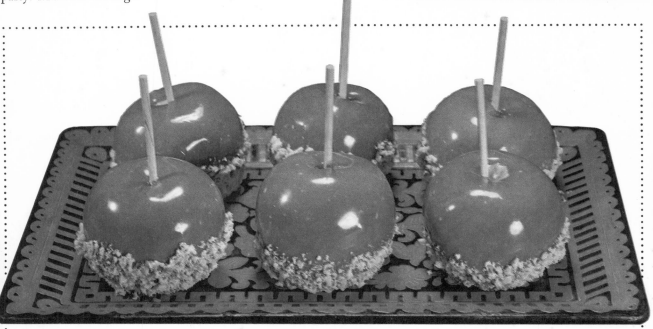

Caramel Apples

Index

A-B

Angel-food cake, 42
Apple-cream coffeecake, 5
Apple pie, fresh, 45
Apples, caramel, 63
Apricot-walnut bread, 3
Baked eggs in cheese
  sauce, 36
Baked macaroni and
  cheese, 36
Baking-powder biscuits, hot, 5
Banana-split pancakes, 57
Barbecued-beef buns, 11
Blanquette de veau, 28
Blueberry muffins, 4
Bread pudding, custard, 50
Bread(s)
  apple-cream coffeecake, 5
  apricot walnut, 3
  baking-powder biscuits,
    hot, 5
  blueberry muffins, 4
  cheese corn crisps, 6
  cheese, wonderful, 8
  corn, criss cross, 4
  hot cross buns, 6
  lemon bubble loaf, 9
  no-knead raisin loaf, 7
  refrigerator rolls, 9
Brown beef stew, 21
Brownie baked Alaska, 56
Buttered carrot sticks, 20

C

Cake(s)
  angel-food, 42
  chocolate roll, 40
  fruit cakelets, 42
  fudge, three-layer, 40
  petal, 43
  sponge, 41
  walnut, 40
  yellow layer, 39
Calico coleslaw, 16
Caramel apples, 63
Caramel-topped custard, 50
Chafing-dish seafood
  Newburg, 35
Charlotte russe supreme, 54
Cheese
  and-onion casserole, 35
  and-rice soufflé, 36
  bread, wonderful, 8
  corn crisps, 6
  pie, strawberry, 48
  soufflé for six, 35
  Swiss pie, 35
Cheesecake, cranberry, 59
Chicken de luxe, creamed, 30
Chicken Tetrazzini, 30
Chocolate
  cinnamon ice cream, 54
  éclairs, 62
  roll, 40
  velvet pie, frozen, 47

walnut drops, double, 38
Chopped coleslaw, 16
Christmas pie, 46
Coleslaw, 16
  calico, 16
  chopped, 16
  dressing, 16
  olive, 16
  Waldorf, 16
Cookies
  brownies, Susan's, 39
  refrigerator, 38
  toffee bars, 39
Corn bread, criss cross, 4
Corn crisps, cheese, 6
Corn sauté, festive, 20
Corned-beef barbecues, 13
Cracker crisp salad, 16
Cranberry-cheesecake, 59
Creamed chicken de luxe, 30
Crème brûlée, 52
Criss cross corn bread, 4
Crowning-glory orange
  soufflé, 52
Custard
  bread pudding, 49
  caramel-topped, 50
  pie, slipped, 45
  pudding, rice, 50

D-E

Desserts
  baked Alaska, brownie, 56
  banana-split pancakes, 57
  caramel apples, 63
  caramel-topped custard, 50
  charlotte russe supreme, 54
  chocolate cinnamon ice
    cream, 54
  cheesecake, cranberry, 59
  crème brûlée, 52
  éclairs, chocolate, 62
  eggs à la neige, 51
  meringue shells à la mode,
    55
  Napoleons, 60
  pudding
    custard bread, 50
    rice custard, 50
    snow, 50
  shortcake, strawberry, 56
  soufflé, crowning-glory
    orange, 52
Deviled eggs, 19
Double chocolate-walnut
  drops, 38
Eclairs, chocolate, 62
Egg(s)
  à la neige, 51
  baked, in cheese sauce, 36
  Benedict, 37
  deviled, 19

F-H-I-L

Fabulous refrigerator rolls, 9
Festive corn sauté, 20
Fillets thermidor, 32
Fillets Veronique, 32
Fish and shellfish
  chowder, 32
  oysters, scalloped, 35
  seafood Newburg, chafing-
    dish, 35
  shrimp creole, 34
  tuna pie, rice-crusted, 33

Fresh apple pie, 45
Frozen chocolate velvet pie, 47
Fruit cakelets, 42
Fudge cake, three-layer, 40
Fudge-nut pie, 45
Hamburger Stroganoff buns,
  11
Hamburger Stroganoff in
  tomato-rice ring, 26
Heavenly pie, 46
Honeyed pineapple-ham loaf,
  26
Hot baking-powder biscuits, 5
Hot corned-beef barbecues, 13
Hot cross buns, 6
How to pare, cut, cube, dice,
  and mince, 14
Ice cream, chocolate
  cinnamon, 54
Lasagna, 37
Lemon bubble loaf, 9
Lemon parfait pie, 44
Lemon pretzel pie, quick, 48
Liver and bacon de luxe, 27

M-N-O

Maraconi and cheese, 36
Meat
  beef stew, brown, 21
  blanquette de veau, 28
  ham loaf, honeyed
    pineapple, 26
  ham loaf, pineapple, 27
  hamburger Stroganoff, 26
  liver and bacon de luxe, 27
  loaf, rainbow, 24
  pie, Mexicali, 22
  pork chops, orange, 27
  pork chops, stuffed, 27
  sukiyaki, 24
Meat-ball pizzas, 23
Melon boat salad, 17
Meringue shells à la mode, 55
Mexicali meat pie, 22
Muffins, blueberry, 4
Napoleons, 60
No-knead raisin loaf, 7
Old-fashioned lettuce bowl,
  16
Olive coleslaw, 16
Orange pork chops, 27
Oysters, scalloped, 35

P-Q-R

Pancakes, banana-split, 57
Party sandwich loaf, 11
Perfect pie shell, 44
Perky raw relishes, 18
Petal cake, 43
Piccalilli, 20
Pie shell, perfect, 44
Pie(s)
  apple, fresh, 45
  cheese, strawberry, 48
  chocolate velvet, frozen, 47
  Christmas, 46
  custard, slipped, 45
  fudge-nut, 45
  heavenly, 46
  lemon parfait, 44
  lemon pretzel, quick, 48
  strawberry cheese, 49
  strawberry tarts, 49
Pineapple-ham loaf, 27
Pinwheel sandwich loaf, 12

Pizzas, meat-ball, 23
Pork chops, orange, 27
Pork chops, stuffed, 27
Potatoes, scalloped, 21
Purple plum ducklings, 31
Quick lemon pretzel pie, 48
Rainbow meat loaf, 24
Refrigerator cookies, 38
Relish(es)
  carrot curls, 18
  celery fans, 18
  cucumber slices, fluted, 18
  olive sticks, 18
  piccalilli, 20
  radish fans, 18
  radish roses, 18
  tray, 18
Rice-crusted tuna pie, 33
Rice custard pudding, 50

S

Salad(s)
  coleslaw, 16
    calico, 16
    chopped, 16
    olive, 16
    Waldorf, 16
  cracker crisp, 16
  lettuce bowl, 16
  melon boat, 17
  potato, skillet, 19
Sandwiches
  barbecued-beef buns, 11
  corned-beef barbecues, 13
  hamburger Stroganoff buns,
    11
  waffle devils, 11
Sandwich loaf, party, 11
Sandwich loaf, pinwheel, 12
Scalloped oysters, 35
Scalloped potatoes, 21
Shrimp creole, 34
Shrimp egg rolls, 2
Skillet potato salad, 19
Slipped custard pie, 45
Snow pudding, 50
Soufflé, cheese-and-rice, 36
Soufflé, crowning-glory
  orange, 52
Soufflé for six, cheese, 35
Spongecake, 41
Strawberry cheese pie, 48
Strawberry shortcake, 56
Strawberry tarts, 49
Stuffed pork chops, 27
Sukiyaki, 24
Susan's brownies, 39
Susan's hashed browns, 21
Swiss pie, 36

T-V-W-Y

Three-layer fudge cake, 40
Toffee bars, 39
Tuna pie, rice-crusted, 33
Turketti, 30
Vegetables
  carrot sticks, buttered, 20
  corn sauté, festive, 20
  hashed browns, Susan's, 21
  scalloped potatoes, 21
Waffle devils, 11
Waldorf coleslaw, 16
Walnut cake, 40
Wonderful cheese bread, 8
Yellow layer cake, 39